A Life Worth Living

Nick Rogen

iUniverse, Inc.
New York   Bloomington

iUniverse books may be ordered through booksellers or by contacting:

iUniverse
1663 Liberty Drive
Bloomington, IN 47403
www.iuniverse.com
1-800-Authors (1-800-288-4677)

ISBN: 978-1-4401-4694-7 (sc)
ISBN: 978-1-4401-4693-0 (dj)
ISBN: 978-1-4401-4695-4 (ebook)

Printed in the United States of America

iUniverse rev. date: 09/17/2009

Contents

Prologue

I was in fifth grade when I first started my suicide watches.

The routine was simple, really. I'd come home early from school (ducking out of participation in local sports), find a new hiding spot for the knives, and watch as Mom crumbled to nothing under the weight of a mental disorder I knew nothing about. While all the other neighborhood kids were busy building model rockets and playing dodge ball, I was doing my best to plead to Mom that her life was worth living.

Yep, that was my life. Other exciting highlights?

- Visiting Mom in "mental hospitals" (where, in fact, they actually do dress all in white) instead of trying out for soccer.

- Straying from conversation with kids at school since my knowledge of pop culture was limited to what medications mixed well together. As one could imagine, I was never really a "hit" at my friend's birthday parties.

- Going to the funerals of Mom's friends who didn't make it. The ones who didn't have a son who hid the knife drawer.

Hell, I was a strong kid, but we all have a breaking point sooner or later, right?

My breaking point came much later, though, at the tail end of my high school stint. It was the usual story of a downfall: drugs, alcohol, hopelessness.

But I'm getting ahead of myself.

I want to tell a story. A horrible, beautiful mess of a story that is different than most. It involves a suicidal mother, drugs, a Switzerland emergency room, more drugs, a fridge won on *The Price Is Right*, even more drugs, a job twisting off bottle caps, a Chinese Wal-Mart, the death of a good friend, and a baby. Sound odd? Believe me, it is. And, unlike other stories about spiraling out of control, this one has a happy ending.

So is the following story about me?

Well, no, not particularly.

This story is really about a small, ten-month-old girl, abandoned and left for dead in the streets of an obscure Chinese village.

This girl is the reason I'm still alive.

And this story is how my family found her.

Or rather, how she found me.

Chapter 1

Home Away from Home (Spring 1996)

"Well." Dad cuts the engine. The classical music we have listened to for two long hours on the drive down to Longview stops. "Here we are."

We've driven down my grandparents' driveway to the back of their aged blue house. Goats and beehives make up the majority of their backyard. Grandpa still makes his own honey as often as his arthritis lets him. In the very corner of the field is a makeshift barn that I doubt has anything of use in it. The empty field coupled with the old barn was the definition of an eleven-year-old's dream.

Only, I wish it was only a dream.

I wish I wasn't here.

I glance to the house beside us. Grandpa smiles and waves from the second floor where their kitchen resides. He stands with an odd arch in his back that I haven't seen before. He had much more hair the last time I saw him, and now his discolored head is almost as bald and shiny as an old, dirty bowling ball. I return only his wave, because smiling is out of the question. I spin around to see that Dad is already gathering my things in the backseat.

"Why can't I stay at home with you?" I ask for what seems like the hundredth time.

He shakes his head and ignores my eyes. "You know the answer."

"How long do I have to stay?" I expect the same response.

He stops collecting my things. His eyes dart over the field and through the trees. He holds back a smirk poorly. "It's not so bad here, you know." Turning to me he says, "Look at your old man! I grew up here for twenty years and look at me now!" He flexes his arm like a bodybuilder.

I laugh, but suck it back in. We both get out and stretch our legs.

"I know it's tough, Nick. If there were any other way, you know I'd be all over it in a heartbeat. And you're old enough to know that I can't watch you all the time." He tugs my backpack out of the car and places it on top of the roof. "The hospitals your mother goes to aren't cheap, and I won't be home much. I'm sorry, I really am, but this is the only way."

I had tried to understand his logic on the way down, but even after the long drive, I still couldn't. "Why don't you just take some time off of work to watch me?"

He sighs. "I wish it was that simple, little buddy."

"It is that simple." I turn away from him.

I want to tell him that I'm hardly a kid anymore. That I'm an adult in every way but my age and both of us know it. I keep my mouth shut though.

Grandma stands in the kitchen now, too. They both appear as though they are waiting to capture me. I love my grandparents, but at this moment it is so easy to imagine them as vultures, waiting to devour me from my family.

"You know, it's only temporary until your mother is back."

I tug at my backpack until it falls off the car roof and into my arms. Dad loads up both his arms with other bags.

"Are you going to visit?" I ask.

"Every chance I get," he says.

I nod. He isn't lying. But I'm not stupid, either. With Mom in the loony bin again and Dad working overtime at Boeing, there will be no one to take care of me.

With all of this happening, I feel so much older than anyone I know. I'm not like everyone else at school. I'm not playing soccer in the playground or darting from dodge balls during recess. Instead, my days consist of leaving school early so I can race home to see if Mom has hurt herself while I was away. That's the kind of life I am living—and that's why I can't understand what Dad means.

"And you can call me anytime you want."

"I will." I slam the car door and follow Dad as he heads toward the house.

"And hey, in case I don't have the chance to tell you"—a smile spreads across his face—"remember that there isn't a whole lot to do at Grandma and Grandpa's for someone your age. So rationalize things. Don't read too many of those Bible tracts they subscribe to or you'll end up like me!"

He laughs at his own joke.

I laugh because it is the only thing I can do to not break down in tears.

Without nothing more to say, we head inside in silence.

Chapter 2

Not Forgotten (Summer 1996)

The grandfather clock above the television set that only receives one channel ticks away the seconds and fills the large room with a rhythmic chant. Grandma sits next to the fireplace, reserved as ever, reading a chapter from her worn Bible. The flames flicker over her face—set so that not even a wrinkle moves. She reminds me of an old Amish woman, like the one from that Harrison Ford movie *Witness*, where he shelters himself in an Amish community to get away from some killers. Grandma has on the same clothes, the same body language—heck, the whole house could have been where the movie was shot!

I look up from the Bible tract I am in the middle of scanning and throw it into the bad pile. Since Dad dropped me off a little over two months ago, I had fully developed a foolproof system to keep from going insane. If a tract was too preachy, too wordy, or didn't have any cool action in it, it went into the "bad" pile, never to be looked at again. If there was any action in it, or even the slightest resemblance of what happened in real life, then off it would go into the "maybe" pile. The "good" pile was reserved for only the best tracts—the ones that reminded me of Saturday morning cartoon strips from the paper. The one about the two klutzy devils trying to convert Christians, for example, was a keeper.

I went through this process daily. Dad wasn't joking, they literally had millions of these things. Tracts are the kind of thing people put in road-stop bathrooms or sneak into unsuspecting mailboxes. How they actually work to show people to Jesus, I can't for the life of me understand. They are the most boring things I've ever seen.

I'm sitting in the middle of the living room, leaning back on the seventies-style green and brown sofa, continuing my sorting. Since it is summer time, and there is no school to keep my interests, this is the only way to busy my days. I don't know any of the kids that live nearby or any parks I can play at.

Yep. It's just me and the tracts.

I gaze over at Grandpa, whose head is tilted back in accordance to the rocking chair he sits in. His mouth hangs open wide like a zombie, while his arms dangle pendulum style from his sides. His snore resembles a chainsaw.

I jump a few feet when the phone rings in the kitchen. Their old phone, which they refuse to replace, sounds like an irritating buzzer that easily wins the award for most annoying sound in the house— barely, over the grandfather clock, of course.

Grandma smiles. "I'll get it," she whispers.

She places her Bible down and moseys to the kitchen.

I look back up at the grandfather clock. It is nearing nine-thirty and Grandma is going to have a small fit with anyone who dares to call this late and interrupt her Bible reading session. Then again, her Bible reading is practically all the time.

After a few minutes, she re-enters the room with a gentle look. Sometimes I wonder if this is what grandmas do all day—wait to hear from people they love and then everything in the world is okay.

When you get as old as Grandma, it seems to me that life becomes just a constant wait for others.

"It's Phillip, your pop, and he wants to talk with you!"

Finally!

I leap up and race to the kitchen. Grandma pats my head as I bound past her. She lets out a chuckle as my socks slip on the polished floor and I smack into the wall that the phone hangs from.

I put the receiver to my ear.

"Hello?" The phone is so old I hope it hasn't disconnected him already.

"Heya buddy!"

"Dad!" I almost lose my grip on the receiver.

"How you holding up down there?" His voice sounds overworked and tired.

"Well, every morning, it's oatmeal. Then in the afternoon, it's the agonizing decision of whether to play with all these old fifties toys of yours or read the Bible tracts."

There is laughter on the other end. "Hey, the pick-up sticks are fun!"

I don't respond.

"Okay, okay. Maybe not." His hearty laugh fills the phone. "So has Grandpa been showing you the shop?"

"Yeah, I've built some pretty cool stuff here. He has everything down in the basement! He has this huge miter saw and this really loud wood polisher! He's even teaching me how to use the router either tomorrow or the next day!" I am so excited that Dad has called that my words are becoming sloppy and rushed. But I don't care.

"That's good. That's real good," he says.

"How are you, Dad?"

"Tired."

All of a sudden, I don't know what else to say. I don't know how to lengthen our conversation without going straight into what I have wanted to ask him since I picked up the phone.

"Dad?"

"Yeah?"

"So am I coming home yet?"

I hear his trademark sigh on the other end. I'm sure he tried to hide it, but it didn't work.

"Actually, your mother is doing much better. I'd say she'll be out in the next week or so. At least that is what the doctors are saying."

I should be happy. But I'm not. I want to be home more than anything in the world. Two months here felt like a year on a deserted island.

"I just want to be home, Dad. I just want everything to be like it used to be. Mom was fine, you'd come home early, we'd build stuff and put up solar panels on the roof and—" I trail off and almost hang up, disappointed that I'm not destined to go home yet. "That's all I really want."

Silence suffocates the line.

"Nick, I ever tell you about the day you were born?"

All the time.

Dad is a modern-day bard, he loves telling stories every chance he gets. Of course, he uses the same ones over and over, but like any good storyteller, he tweaks them just enough, so subtly that you can't even pinpoint the difference. This way they end up sounding unique each and every time.

"I don't remember," I fib.

"When your mother woke me up that morning and told me she needed to go the hospital, I panicked. I ran around the room like a raped ape." I break out into laughter. Dad always has the cleverest similes that make absolutely no sense. "So there I was, knocking things over left and right and I ended up knocking over the bedside lamp and suddenly this burst of fire illuminated the room and the sheets on the bed were covered in flames."

Grandma has walked into the kitchen and pulled a pan out from the stove. My eyes are full of tears I am laughing so hard. I can hardly see her through the blur.

"So your mother is screaming. I'm screaming. And I'm beating pillows on the bed like I'm playing a giant Congo drum. Anyway, I

7

stop the flames and we head to the hospital. And everything is fine and dandy as you were being delivered until suddenly, you just stopped."

"Stopped?" I can barely manage to respond.

"Yep, you just stopped. You just wouldn't come out any farther than halfway. Pushing didn't help any. So the doctor gets out—I'm not kidding you—this plunger and attaches it to your tiny little head. And he just starts yanking on you like he's unclogging a toilet."

"No way! A plunger?"

"A plunger! I swear! No lie! So finally, the doctor plunges you out and puts you in your mother's arms. She does the whole *oooohh* and *ahhhh* thing and then places you in my arms. And I hate to say it, but you had to be the ugliest baby I had ever seen. You were all black and blue, bruised up from all the plunging. You even had a cone-shaped head! I remember looking at your mother and being so angry at her for bearing such an ugly child."

I grab my side. Every time I hear the story, everyone around who isn't in our family looks confused about whether or not to laugh. A parent laughing about how ugly he found his kid to be is not something very many people find funny. But it is my family's dark and morbid humor that keeps us going, and I know he always turns it around to make the ending a good one.

"I mean, I thought you'd end up in one of those special education classes your mother taught. When I walked you down to the birthing unit, I felt ashamed of how ugly you were! And it took a couple of days until your head finally went back to normal. Man, it was bad."

He goes silent and waits until my laughter subsides.

"Man, I love that story," I say.

"But the thing is, Nick." His voice is back to the tired, serious tone he had when he first called. "I shouldn't have ever felt ashamed because you turned out to be the most beautiful kid I've ever known. You turned out to be every father's dream."

I swallow hard. "Thanks, Dad."

"That's the part of the story you need to remember most—" He sighs. "I'll get you home as soon as I can kiddo. I promise you that."

"I know."

"I love you, little buddy."

"I love you too, Dad."

He coughs. "Can you put Grandpa on the phone? Wake him for me?"

"Yeah, it'll just be a second. Bye, Dad."

With renewed energy, I set the receiver down and go wake up Grandpa. It won't be much longer, and I'll be home again and everything will be back to normal.

I just know it.

Everything will be okay.

Chapter 3

Lost and Found (February 2003)

By the time the secretary at the desk calls my name, my long legs are shaking so rapidly I feel I should be seeing the doctor about the early onset of Parkinson's. Sweat clings to my back. I set down the magazine I'm not actually reading.

The waiting room is pretty full for a Thursday afternoon. Four kids are playing in the children's corner, running around on what looks a lot like a sugar high. Their shrill screams tip their parent's heads in dismay.

Maybe the doctor won't give me anything.

I watch a child bounce around with a Game Boy, punching and kicking with every mash of a button.

I mean, should I really be here? I'm not like any of these kids.

"Nicholas?" The nurse that pops out from behind the doctor's door is patient. She probably deals with distracted individuals all day.

"Yeah?"

"You can go on back, Nicholas. The doctor is ready for you." Her voice rises as she speaks in competition with the sugar children.

I thank the secretary and greet the casually dressed doctor who comes out of nowhere with a hand extended toward me.

"Hey there, Nicholas!" I can hear the Spanish accent in his words even though he looks American. His teeth are white as pearls. Like every rich doctor. "Good to see you! Your dad has told me quite a few stories about you over the years!"

His handshake is firm. My own is no match, crushing under his strength.

"All good I hope."

He takes my shoulder and guides me to a room on his right. "All good I swear! Right this way."

I sit down on a couch opposite his desk and am flanked by fake trees. The small coffee table in front of me is bare except for a tissue box and a Mother Mary statue in the center. The doctor sits down in his swivel chair and rustles through a pile of papers on his desk. My eyes waver to the wall behind him where an organized collage of degrees of various sorts line the entire wall.

Typical.

Why is it that doctors feel the need to show off their education?

I'm not a fan of doctors of any sort. None of them have ever helped Mom. They always nod their head, blindly write some random prescription in that illegible doctor handwriting of theirs, and send her on her suicidal way. How helpful, huh? To Mom, that's what doctors were for; to get the meds that you had researched for yourself. Sadly, the carelessness of doctors made it so the patients had the responsibility to find the right combination of medication.

Myself? I'd always seen it as a bleak way to look at doctors—pill dispensers with degrees. But here I am, doing the same thing. Here just to push back the Pez head to get the candy.

"So." He looks up from his paperwork. "You believe you have Attention Deficit Disorder?"

I laugh. "Geez, after my last month? Yeah. I've locked my keys in my car three times in one week. Heck, I even have the locksmith's personal cell phone number for the next time it happens." I take out my wallet and the card the locksmith had given me and wave it in the air. "Said I was putting his kids through college."

The doctor chuckles.

"Seriously though, my attention span seems to be getting less and less the older I get. I can't keep track of anything anymore. I feel like my brain is going a thousand different directions all at once."

The doctor begins to scribble on his papers as he talks. "Well ADD can be genetic, especially in males. And I don't think I have to remind you how bad your dad was before he came to me!"

"We must have hit a dozen mailboxes when I was kid because he couldn't pay attention to the road—" I laugh and realize I'm not joking.

"Any problems in school?"

"Gradewise? No, but I'm halfway through my junior year now and the more responsibility I'm getting, the harder it is to focus on simple things."

To be honest, I can't tell if I'm lying to him, and the truth of the matter was quite simple. I had taken one of Dad's Adderall pills one day before school. I saw the wonders it had done for Dad and thought that maybe I could have the same result. I honestly thought that the pills could help me find the direction I didn't have in my life. All I needed was a little jumpstart.

Maybe this pill was the answer.

Maybe it would tell me what to do after high school.

Maybe it would help me write.

Ah, to write. My one childhood dream I still kept fresh, to become a writer. The only problem? I never got the courage to actually do the writing.

So, I took Dad's pill and my mind exploded—in words, in ideas, in everything. I sat down and wrote for hours. I came up with a plot and everything. I was Bradbury with a slight push. Was I really ADD or was it just the side effects of "legalized speed"? Whatever it was, it made me feel good, and it made me able to write, and that was all that mattered.

"Uh hum," is all the doctor says. He scribbles a few more things down before talking again. "What you're describing to me sounds like the classic case of a mild version of Attention Deficit Disorder. Given your dad has it as well, though more of the hyperactive end, it makes it quite a bit easier to diagnosis it in you." He scribbles even more. Is he actually writing something or just drawing pictures? "I'm going to start you out on ten milligrams a day of Adderall HR, the same medication your father is on. We'll see how that dosage works out for the next couple months and go from there."

What?

He stops writing and looks up with a smile. "And you're all done!"

I don't know how easy it is to steal candy from a baby, but this has to be easier. I get up and try to not look too surprised. We exchange good-byes, and I head for my car.

The whole ordeal didn't last more than ten minutes.

⤳

Driving out of the pharmacy lot, I reach for the bag on my passenger's seat. I rip open the paper bag and take out the bottle inside. I alternate glances from the road to the directions on the side of the bottle. It tells me to take one ten-milligram capsule every morning.

I screw off the bottle top and dry-swallow three. I place the bottle back in the bag. I feel a sort of guilt sweep over me as I drive home, but as the drug begins to take effect, I'm able to ignore it the rest of the way.

Everything will make sense now. I've found the answer I'm looking for.

I'm sure of it.

Chapter 4

Flight from Hell (July 2003)

I lay my head on the window, and for the first time in days I am able to close my eyes and fall asleep.

The hallway that is before me is dressed in white. It has a "tunnel to the afterlife" vibe to it.

But this isn't the afterlife.

I'm dreaming.

Wake up, Nick. Wake up, you're having a dream.

Suddenly I'm moving, or gliding, I can't really tell. The walls scroll by. Up ahead, an elderly nurse waves me through a suddenly open door with a smile. I try to smile back but the dream doesn't let me.

When I pass the doorway, I feel a flash of color that is indescribable. Then again, how does one describe a color? It's cold and black even though the walls are still pure and white. Does that make sense?

It doesn't matter.

I try to pinch myself awake.

Wake up, Nick.

It doesn't work.

Now there are doors on both my sides. My pace slows. Most of them remain closed as I pass, but others creak open. I peer into them with curiosity.

In one, a man rocks back and forth in the corner of the room, his lips twisting into ugly shapes as he shouts obscenities. Another room has a mad dash of male nurses holding down a screaming patient.

One produces a needle, holds it up in front of their eyes and squirts out some of the juice inside. It's just like what they do in the movies for effect—to scare the audience. To get the audience to think it only happens in the movies.

Another room has a man talking to a wall. Maybe he's having a dream too, but I doubt it.

Wake up. Please. Wake up now.

Another door opens. The room is simple, only a single bed and no décor. On it sits a beautiful, middle-aged woman, her hands digging into her blonde curly hair. She is crying and shaking.

I turn and enter the room and bend down so I can see her better.

She lifts her head. Empty, zombie eyes stare back. The skin around her eyes is red like licorice. Her tears are mascara black and leave a wiggly vein down her pearly skin.

She's like an angel.

Like a mother.

Like *my* mother.

"Hi," I whisper. Somehow, I know all along this is the person I am here to visit, and this is the last place I want to be.

Wake up, Nick.

She sniffles and asks me what I'm doing in her room.

"I've come to visit you, Mom."

Who are you? She asks me without moving her mouth.

"It's Nick, Mom. Your son." I can see my reflection in her eyes. I look like a wreck. My red hair is tangled and my skinny face looks as pale as a skeleton.

Her body suddenly launches up and I back away.

My mother is no longer crying.

Leave, she says, or I'll call a nurse.

I try to calm her. She pushes me away.

Now I'm crying. And I never cry.

My body feels heavier. Gravity has intensified and I fall to my knees. The pull to the ground is too strong for me to ignore. My blood is made of iron.

Oh God. Is this real? Is this a dream?

Wake up, Nick. Wake up, dammit!

I put my head down. Everything is blurry through my tears. The white walls around me are swirling into the black and being swallowed whole.

I hear a whisper at my ear.

"You can't be her son. Look at you! You're a wreck! How could she ever be proud of you?"

It's not my mother talking this time. This time, the voice is my own.

I try to wipe my tears and see that I'm shaking and sweating.

I suddenly feel so high I'm ashamed.

I look up. My mother's face is putty. *The Invasion of the Body Snatchers.* They've got her. This isn't my mother. It couldn't be.

Time has stopped.

"I can save you!" I scream.

Her mouth contorts to a wicked smile.

You did save me, her still lips say, but what good is that if my own son can't save himself?

I close my eyes.

She's right. You are a failure.

What a waste of a good life.

It's the last thing I hear from my dream mother.

Wake up, Nick.

I finally do.

⤸

I wrench myself out of my seat and gasp for air. The seatbelt slams me back. I close my eyes and try to calm myself.

It was a dream! Just a dream! Calm down! Calm down, Nick!

My heart is breaking through my ribs.

"So much for sleep," I wheeze to the empty plane seat next to me.

∽

The rest of the plane ride is uneventful to say the least. My small nap occurred about an hour after take-off, which means we still have a good thirteen hours until touchdown in Amsterdam.

We're passing over Washington DC now, right above a lightning storm. I watch as every bolt takes form before it shoots to the world below.

My shakes are dying down.

A whole month in Europe.

A whole month without Adderall.

A whole month to regain who I was before getting addicted.

I laugh and a man sitting in the aisle across from me looks my way. I lean back and smile. I must look crazy.

What a dramatic seventeen-year-old!

Mom's illness made it so we never had any family trips. Well, unless family outings to the local mental institution equaled Disneyland. They sure as hell weren't a theme park though. There weren't any "you must be this tall to ride" signs to ward off the small kids.

Sometimes, I wish there were.

But that was all in the past. Mom was medicated now. Stable. We could finally go on that well-deserved vacation. So, we packed our backpacks, charted a course, and were ready to trek across Europe on our own.

I'm ecstatic. Not only for the new world I am about to experience, but it is going to be a full month without pills.

Ah, the pills.

The Adderall did help my writing. I had half a novel under my belt.

But I'd become so reliant on the drug that I took it like candy. It was a crutch and I was tired of using it.

I can become the writer I want without a drug.

This month will be proof of that.

Proof I am a good kid.

And proof that I am someone who can make my mother proud.

⤿

I've been nodding in and out of REM sleep for hours now. A few seconds here. A few stolen moments there. Nothing concrete though. Not real sleep. My body is a wreck; an endless battle between old chemicals and the demand for sleep.

Neither side is winning.

I wrestle in my chair.

God, how long have I been on this plane? I check my watch. Three in the morning, according to my old, Seattle time.

But, of course, the sun outside the plane is oozing through the cracks of my window curtain. Why they never make the curtain larger than the exact window size is beyond me. It's doing nothing to block out the brightness of the sun.

I rub my eyes. My body aches, bones crack. I try to close my eyes and settle my oddly beating heart.

It just isn't happening.

Some start for a vacation, uh?

And without notice, I fall asleep.

⤿

I'm woken up by the overhead announcement that we're to land in Amsterdam in a matter of minutes.

"Arg—" I groan and grab my head. It throbs, the veins thumping like a heart into my hand.

The pain spikes. It's so intense I feel like my head is going to explode.

This isn't withdrawal. This is something else.

Something worse.

Oh God, I'm dying aren't I?

Dad's side of the family always had notoriously bad hearts. I'm sure my intake of a copious amount of legal speed these last few months hasn't helped.

The pain surges again.

I gasp out the only prayer I can think of.

"Now I lay me down to sleep, I pray the Lord my soul to keep. And if"—I pant. The plane around me is blurring. I try my best to continue—"I should die before I wake, I pray the Lord my soul to take."

I bury my head in my hands and crumple up in the seat.

What in God's name is happening to me?

As quick as it came, the sudden surge of pain stops. The plane is descending and losing altitude. I keep a hold of my head for a few more minutes before the pain is only a dull pounding.

I wipe the tears splattered and smashed against my face. No one around me has noticed a thing.

My stomach is on tumble.

Everything is in complete vertigo.

When the plane stops, I make no effort to get up until everyone is gone. I take my time getting my backpack from the overhead compartment. The airplane attendant follows me out.

I meet up with Jordan, my good friend who came along for the European Adventure, and my parents outside the terminal.

They're chatting up a storm.

"Look at the architecture!" they say.

"Look at the people!" they whisper.

"What a culture shock!" they continue to repeat out loud.

I stay silent. My head can't even begin to keep up with them.

It is afternoon in the Netherlands by the time we exit onto the crowded streets. We make our best effort to head to the hostel we booked last week on our own. There are maps in all of our hands.

Like my dream, I glide alongside them until we find our hostel. The tiny man takes our money and leads us up a staircase out of a horror movie. I lose track of steps after the fiftieth.

When we get to our room, I crash into the bed, literally, and fall instantly to sleep.

Jet lag, a mysterious headache of death, and a killer array of stimulant withdrawals—my life is never, ever boring.

Chapter 5

Amsterdam

We spend the next few days touring the outskirts of Amsterdam.

My headaches, shakes, and other withdrawal symptoms have slowly begun to lessen. My energy, however, is still nonexistent; having gone from being energized all the time to being weak and tired. It's hard and I try my best to stay with the group.

Amsterdam is like Gotham City on acid. It has cobblestone roads and endless nightlife (the music from the nightclub below our hostel room vibrates the walls at night). It also reminds me of a livelier New York. People seem to be everywhere. Though there are still cars here, the majority of people walk or ride bikes. I must have taken over a dozen shots with my throwaway camera of the "bicycle garages" that litter the streets. There are more bikes in one three-level garage than there are in all the Tours de France combined.

We rent bikes of our own so we can explore the outskirts of the city, which are lined with knee-high grass and windmills. It's a Don Quixote dream.

I spend most of my time writing in the journal I brought over from the States. I scribble down everything I see and feel. My inspiration took a hit when I stopped taking Adderall, but I try my best to write even if I don't want to.

While passing the time in a hostel waiting room, I watch a Danish youth across from me scribbling away in his journal.

Is he writing down his culture shock as well? Or is he like me? Practicing to be a writer?

I don't ask and continue to write.

⟿

A writer.

That's what I say when someone asks me what I want to be when I grow up.

A writer, I say.

When Mom was sick, Dad was always working. I was a shy kid with less than a handful of close friends. I had a lot of friends, don't get me wrong, but they were only school friends. Kind of hard to tell someone, "Yeah, let's hang out! I just got to hide the knife set in case my Mom tries to hurt herself. Oh, and that constant crying all night? Just ignore it! We'll have a great slumber party!"

So I wrote. I was never too good at expressing my own feelings. I'm still not too good at it. But I'm a masterful metaphor builder. I wrote ten page stories about a crime fighter who fought pain. Fought disease. He fought everything I wished I could. I sold each one for five bucks a pop.

They sure were shitty.

And Mom bought every single issue.

So maybe, initially, I have Mom to thank for pushing me to be a writer.

I just wish I knew where that inspiration went.

Wish I knew the moment I stopped believing in myself and stopped in fear of failure.

Almost a full year of being on Adderall and I wrote half a book. I'm proud of that, but I'm not proud that I had to abuse the drug to squeeze the inspiration from me.

So now, I have a whole continent as my canvas and I sure as hell am going to put it to good use.

Chapter 6

My Van Gogh Mother

"You'll like this one," Mom promises me.

I laugh as we enter the line outside the gothic stone building.

"The last one, that Rijksmuseum, almost kicked me back into a deep depression it was so boring."

Mom grins. Since she's better now, we laugh at how it used to be, before she got on the right medication. Morbid as it is, we try to make light of everything. It's our survival technique. Take nothing too seriously.

"Van Gogh is different," she says.

"Different how?" I ask. "Well, except for the fact he had one less ear."

"Apparently he's bipolar as well. Or was."

"Right," I say as I lift my shirt and dig through my money belt for some change. "But you're bipolar, too, and you didn't cut off your ear and give it as a gift it to a prostitute."

She chuckles and doesn't respond.

∽

I walk through the museum like a ghost, speaking to no one. I read all the history of Van Gogh's life scribbled on the walls.

I soak him in and feel his anger as he paints and describes how the church pushed him away because he lived with the poor people.

Originally, he was going to pursue a career in the Catholic Church. But they "banished" him for getting too close to the people he was trying to save. Pretty fucked up, eh?

I understand his slow descent into madness. Or what many believe was depression. By the end of his life, he was utterly alone. He was a failure as an artist, only selling one painting during his entire life, and that was to his sister who felt sorry for him.

It isn't until I reach the painting titled *At Eternity's Gate* that I stop completely. A rush of sadness overwhelms me. The man in the picture is tired. At the end of his rope. His tiny, bald head is smothered by his hands, which are clenched into fists of rage, as if it is the opposite of a man in prayer. As though he is furious with God. The picture doesn't show his face and a part of me is glad it doesn't.

I can't help but think this is the true Van Gogh self portrait. A sad, little man sitting on a dilapidated chair.

A quote from Van Gogh is nearby, painted on the wall.

It reads: "I feel ... failure. This is my destiny, which I accept and which will never change."

The quote is Medusa. I'm mesmerized. Stuck in place. I write the quote down in my journal and circle it.

I'm speechless by the time I get to the museum's café.

Poor Van Gogh. Had he had the medical treatment and diagnosis we have now, would he have been helped? Would it have stopped him from pulling that shotgun trigger?

The rest of my group is already sitting in the café. I see Mom from a distance and feel happy again.

What would have happened if Mom hadn't gotten help? Would she have gone the same route?

Thank God I don't ever have to answer those questions.

I sit down at the table. I'm ready to burst with excited chatter about the museum's beauty, but stop myself when I notice Mom's eyes are glossy and tears are scrolling down her face.

And my heart sinks.

~

"Mom? Mom? What's wrong?" I'm in protector mode.

She sucks in a breath.

"Mom's not doing too well, Nick," Dad answers for her. "Why don't you go get some food? I'm sure you're starving."

I look to Jordan. He stares outside. I look back to Mom and she makes an effort not to make eye contact.

"Alright," I say.

As I go down the aisle of lunch options, I try to not look back at our table. I feel like ordering a "this-can't-be-happening" meal with a side of "disbelief."

When I return, Mom has started to cry louder.

We leave our food half-eaten and ask the front desk where the nearest hospital is. The man marks it on our map with a large circled H.

We pedal through the rainy streets like hell was behind us.

Once, when I was a kid, something similar to this happened. We were vacationing in Portland, and Mom's body shut down; an intense "mystery" heat burning through her. We took the latest train home that night. They got us a compartment for free since they didn't want Mom's moans and cries to scare the other passengers. When we got home, we tried to sleep it off. It didn't work. We headed to the ER right in time. Mom melted down. She wailed about how horrible of a mother she was and how life would be better for me if she wasn't around.

I held her hand as they injected her with sedatives.

The next day they tried her on a new drug that was out on the market. It was like Lazarus back from the dead. It proved to me that maybe God had listened to my prayers. She had been better ever since.

The storm hitting Amsterdam is fierce. Rain pelts at us as we dip through the cars and motorcycles in the city square. Mom looks liked a wet, ownerless dog.

In the rain, at least you can't see Mom's tears.

Or mine. And like I said, I never cry.

The demons of the past are coming back and I don't know what to do.

When we arrive, we rush to the waiting room. It looks no different than an American ER; only the constant buzz and chatter of nurses and other patients speaking in Dutch tells us how far we really are from home.

So far, yet the same problems follow.

Odd how life works.

We all take a seat and I try to stay collected as Mom leaves with a nurse.

Oh, please God. Not again.

I'm shaking and it's not because of the rain.

Everything seems so familiar. I close my eyes and sleep grabs ahold.

Chapter 7

Shock Therapy

I shouldn't have closed my eyes. Sometimes memories are like Polaroid pictures. The picture of Mom's first electroshock therapy is fading back into view, and I'm suddenly eleven-years-old again.

The walls are the same plain white. The chairs are all the same; stained wood with flowery cushioning. The receptionist sits behind a glass wall, typing away at her computer while talking loudly with someone on the phone. In front of me on the table are the typical adult magazines that hold no interest for me. Really, the only difference in this room compared to all the others is that there are no toys. No rainbow-colored assortment of Legos to keep children entertained or any magazines to color in.

Does this place even have kids?

I shouldn't be here. I know that much.

I look around while staying as quiet as I can in my oversized chair. Across the room sits a man who looks much younger than Dad. I watch him closely.

He flips through a magazine slowly. His eyes stare straight into the page, as though he is having a staring contest and is intent on winning. But he isn't reading. In fact, he's not doing anything at all.

I turn to Dad, who is right next to me. His hands crossed, his body leaned forward, head bowed down. I bet if I could see his eyes, he would have had the same blank expression as the man across the room.

I make a mental note to write this down when I get home. It would be a perfect enemy for my next story.

The enemy: Despair.

After some time, Dad's head rises. He looks over to me and attempts a grin but fails. "Won't be too much longer, little buddy—"

"Anyone ever tell you that you look like Ned Flanders from *The Simpsons*?" I blurt out. It is the only thing I can think to say.

He lets out a belly laugh that only my Dad can produce. "No. Do I sound like him?"

"Well, no," I admit.

"Well okaly-dokaly then. That's good!"

My laughter fills in for the kids who aren't here. Who are off playing with toys. Who are off living their children lives.

He bows his head again and my laughter dies off quickly. Maybe this isn't a time for jokes or laughter. After all, there is nothing funny here.

Instead of another joke, I ask what has been on my mind the whole afternoon. "Is Mom going to be okay?"

He looks up and rubs my head. I've never seen Dad so tired in all my life. "She'll be fine." He pauses. "She's going to act a little funny for the next couple days and she'll need your help."

"Because of the shock treatment?" I had heard him use the term with Mom before. They had been arguing in the kitchen a few nights ago after they thought I had fallen asleep. They were arguing about the risk of doing the treatment.

I looked up in the dictionary that night to see what it was.

e·lec·tro·con·vul·sive therapy (ĭ-lĕk'trō-kən-vŭl'sĭv) n. Abbr. ECT Administration of electric current to the brain through electrodes placed on the head in order to induce seizure activity in the brain, used in the treatment of certain mental disorders, especially severe depression. Also called electroshock therapy.

Inducing a seizure in the brain for relief? It was like something out of a bad science fiction movie.

Dad's eyes sink and I can no longer tell him apart from the man across from me. "Yes. Because of the shock treatment. At first her memory will be a bit fuzzy, so just make sure you're there to help her when she needs it."

"But she'll just forget the small stuff, right. Like where we live and stuff? Isn't that why we're here? Because she can't drive home by herself?" I know I had asked too many questions, but I also know that Dad will answer all of them truthfully. He never skirts past anything I ever ask him or changes the subject. Dad always tells me the truth, and I love him for that.

"Yes."

But today, he doesn't say anymore.

⤳

"Hi." Mom's voice sounds flat. It's almost as though her words don't belong to her, as though they aren't even coming from her mouth. There is no ring to them. In fact, there is no tone at all.

A robot voice.

She smiles at me from the doctor's door. I try to smile back but can't. Even her smile looks fake; practiced in the mirror before being shown in public. Her eyes look dead; blue as the ocean, but void of any of the manic emotion that was such a prominent characteristic of my mother.

I get up and run to her. I dig my head into her side and squeeze as hard as I can. When she hugs back, I finally discover some warmth about her. At least something is right here. No matter what, she is still my mother.

~

"Nick?"

I open my eyes with a gasp. My body is sticky and cold.

I should have brought some Adderall, even just a little, just to ease off it slowly. Cold turkey may not have been the way to go. My energy is so low, I fall asleep without control.

Dad is shaking my shoulder. "Nick? Mom's back. We can go now."

"What was it? Did they give her anything?"

He shakes his head. "They haven't got a clue what's happening to her."

Dad's brutal honesty again.

Funny. Fly halfway across the world and doctors are the same here. They don't know a damn thing.

We all leave the hospital in worse shape than when we had arrived.

Chapter 8

Switzerland

We leave the laid-back streets of Amsterdam a day later. Mom's bipolar "rapid cycling" appears to be back in full swing after all these years. Today, thank God, she seems to be back to normal.

I pray she lasts through the trip this way.

In our marijuana-smelling room, we chart a course on our large European map for Switzerland. Lush mountains filled with gorgeous rolling hills. How can anyone resist that?

We snatch the Eurail and I ride between two large Danish women who talk the entire way to Bern, our stopover. We nab an overnight car and sleep our way through the border.

This isn't the Hilton. We don't have money to spend on fancy hotels or rooms, so we sleep in our regular train seats.

It's the most uncomfortable sleep I've ever had.

We arrive at Interlaken, Switzerland, sleep-deprived and red-eyed.

The town is beautiful. The mountains truly do mist around me. They're green and expansive. It's like being trapped in a bowl—a 360-degree mountain range that rivals anything seen in *The Lord of the Rings*.

It's the definition of a dream.

I'm happy to be alive.

To be free of Adderall.

Mom is better, at least for the moment, and my last year of high school is before me. On top of all this, I have plenty of inspiration to keep writing.

I gotta say, it doesn't get any sweeter than this.

⌒

Craig grins over at me. His young face shines.

"Hell yeah, Nick! I'm glad to hear that. More kids your age have to get out here. Travel! See the world! 'Cause let me tell you, the world isn't coming to you. You have to go after the world!"

I stretch out in my bunk bed and nod Craig's way. He slowly packs his bag and makes his bed across from me.

"It's only been a week and I feel—" I stutter.

He places a canteen into his pack and looks over.

"Alive?"

"Yeah," I agree.

It's silent in our room for the first time since we came to The Backpacker's Villa just outside the main town drag. Jordan and my parents are out exploring. I got caught up talking with our roommate who's been here for over a week now. Craig is a fellow American, sifting his way around Europe to find himself. He's charismatic and talkative. The kind of guy who can get you to spill your life's ambitions to him and not even realize you're doing it.

"Alive, huh? So why do you think that is, Nick?"

Here he goes with the soul-digging questions.

I cave in with ease.

"I guess"—I try to make sure I think before I start speaking—"I guess I realized that when I get out of high school, I can't work in a cubicle job. You know, that job that makes you hit the snooze button on your alarm. The job that makes you get four extra shots in your mocha to get through the day. The kind of job that doesn't allow for a window because they don't want you to dream about anything outside the cubicle. And all you do it for is the money. Screw money!"

I stop. *Where's this anger about money coming from?*

Craig just shows more teeth.

With the stage still set, I continue. "I want a job where I wake up every day and say, 'God I can't wait to start this day!'"

"Yeah? And what job is that?"

"I don't know. Maybe a writer or something."

Craig zips his backpack and gives me a curious look. "A writer? Hmmmm—"

Silence again.

"Why a writer?"

I attempt to answer but the words stop at my lips.

Why do I want to be a writer?

"I don't know."

The answer I give him disturbs me. Sure, I'd always been good at writing and Mom encouraged me, but the more I thought about it, the more I realized I didn't even know why it was my dream.

Craig notices my silence.

"You'll figure out the answer soon enough. Trust me."

He lurches his massive bag over his shoulder and starts buckling it to his chest.

"So where are you off to Craig?" I change topics.

"Nick," he laughs, "I haven't had a real job, those cubicle jobs you were talking about, in years. My current job is climbing those Alps." He points out the window to the largest peak. "Pay's not too great, and no hazard pay or insurance to boot. But you know, it really makes me feel—"

He stops mid-sentence and dashes out the door.

I lay back and soak in the summer rays that filter through my window.

"Alive," I finish his sentence to the empty room, close my eyes, and drift into a sound sleep.

⌒

I wake up to my heart bursting through my chest. My throat is burning, every gulp a large coal trickling down like a slug. I use my shaky hands to wipe off the thick layer of sweat pooling on my forehead. I feel my head thump in my hands.

Plane ride mystery headache, part two.

Great.

I can't hear out my left ear. Something is very wrong.

It's nighttime now and the room is dark; a dash of the moon shining into the window. I get up and take care not wake anyone. Jordan is passed out with half of his body in the bed and half lying on the floor. Dad is buried in every pillow he could find. Craig's bed is untouched.

I creep outside to the main hallway and to the bathroom. I flip the switch and my eyes light on fire.

Looking back at me in the mirror is a mess. Green, bloodshot eyes, ghost skin, an unshaven face. Like a wild night in Amsterdam.

My left ear is now ringing.

"It's nothing, Nick. You'll be fine in the morning," I tell myself.

I crawl back to bed and am out in a matter of minutes.

⌒

I sleep through the entire next day.

When I finally wake up, I feel much better. The group is heading into the mountains to a town called Grindelwald.

I'm happy to tag along.

We take a tram that speeds up the mountain as though it were a miniature model. The trees, the houses; they all look so unreal. So perfect. Like a photograph that moves.

We hike up to the top of the nearest mountain outside Grindelwald and have a short lunch. Everything is like a dream.

It's not until the way down that everything amazing about the trip comes crashing down.

Chapter 9

Things Don't Look Good

Cue mystery planeride illness finale.

I lean my body into the train window as it descends the mountain slower than it seemed going up. I push my head to the glass and hope that somehow, if I push hard enough, the less my head will feel the need to explode.

A transfer of energy. Too bad it doesn't work that way.

"Oh God," I mumble. I can't even hear myself. My ears are so plugged up that the world around me is drowning underwater.

Mom mouths a sentence toward me to decipher.

I groan in response.

She repeats louder. "We'll get you to a hospital the second we get back to the hostel, alright?"

I nod and close my eyes.

Why does this keep happening to me? Am I dying?

The next twenty minutes drag. When the tram finally stops, I stumble out behind Mom.

"Mom? Can we just go to the hospital and let Jordan and Dad go back to the hostel? I don't think I can walk all the way there and then back."

"Of course," she says. We say our good-byes and head toward the middle of the town.

We don't talk.

It's almost funny, I realize. The roles of mother and son are reversed.

Mother takes care of son now. Back to normal. Back to what it should be. Back to—

Shut the hell up Nick. I curse to myself for the insensitive thoughts.

It's getting darker in the sky and every store we pass has long since closed shop. We pass a single resident on the street.

"Hospital?" We both ask in unison.

"What?" The man replies in rough English.

"Hospital?" Mom asks in her loudest voice. He's foreign, not deaf, but the raised voice seems to get the point across.

"Ah, hospital!" He points further down the road, smiles, and continues on his way.

I start to laugh. "That was the least helpful directional advice I've ever heard!"

Mom smiles. I'm glad she's with me.

We trek in the direction the man pointed out for us. Soon, we've walked out of the actual town and are strolling through the residential neighborhood. It's fancy and upscale. Like a Hollywood neighborhood. The only difference is that the mountains in the distance look like odd cutouts in the fading sunlight.

By the time we find the hospital, it is forty-five minutes later, and the day is completely gone. We struggle to find the ER, as the signs don't seem to contain any English at all.

The emergency room is empty. Calm. A blonde woman in a short miniskirt approaches us.

"Hi. My son here needs a doctor. Something is wrong with his ears. He can't hear out of them. It's probably an infection or something."

The nurse stares and nods.

Great.

Her face scrunches up. She holds up a finger to signal us to wait. She turns and rushes out of the lobby.

"This outta be interesting," I say to Mom.

A few minutes pass before another nurse appears. She looks exactly like nurse number one. She's smiling, too. In fact, she doesn't stop.

Mom repeats her words.

The nurse loses her smile.

"English?" I interrupt.

Her head bounces and she says, "English!"

She tilts her head and points to her own ear. "Ear?"

I nod like a madman. Give this nurse a prize!

"Ah, ear. Ear." She's smiling again. "Follow."

We stay near to her as she leads us to a closed-off room and sits me down in a chair in the middle of the room. She hands over a clipboard of papers for Mom to fill out.

The nurse takes the usual. Blood pressure. Heart beat. Stick-in-the-mouth-say-ah. Finally she gets down to business and checks my ears.

"Sound?"

"No, it's like I'm underwater."

"Ah," she says in that not-understanding tone. "Tell what happened."

Ugh.

"Plane ride over here, my head hurt." I point to my head. "And my ears." I point to my ears. I've learned very quickly that gestures are the universal language. "Plugged."

"Plugged?"

"Ah, ah, no … no sound."

"Ah."

"And they were fine until I went up the mountains." I make a triangle with my hands and point up. I'm getting pretty good at this interpreter stuff. "And they just popped."

Her face scrunches up.

"Popped, ah—" I stumble on my words and decide to cut to the chase. "Need antibiotic."

"Antibyeahtic?" She struggles to say the word.

"Uh, pills," I say.

She smiles.

It's all about the right wording.

She leaves and Mom looks up from her paperwork. "You know how hard it was for me not to laugh at that little exchange of culture just now?"

"Hey, I tried. I can't help that I'm an ignorant American who doesn't know any other language."

The nurse reenters the room with a tiny spray bottle and a white pill box. She hands them to me and I thank her.

"Antibiotics?" I try again.

She doesn't answer, but instead takes the forms from Mom and begins to flip through them to see if everything is filled out.

I examine the pill box and realize I can't make out even a single word. Not even a recognizable number jumps out to me.

I hold them up to the nurse. "How many?" I start to count.

She stops me at two and smiles and nods. "Yes, two."

"Alright." I groan and hope she understood my question.

She puts the clipboard down and addresses both of us. "More pills. Not here. We go there now. Taxi."

Right. I don't even try to respond.

The nurse beckons us to follow and leads us to a taxi cab outside.

We thank her and get inside.

"Some night this is turning out to be," I say to Mom.

"Never boring."

The taxi man turns his pudgy head. "Americans, eh?"

I almost fall off my seat.

"Yeah, yeah, from Washington state."

"Good to hear. Good to hear indeed. We don't get too many Americans here since the war started. Must've been hell in that ER. Even their official translator can't really speak a lick of English." He coughs a New York cough, deep and powerful. "In case they didn't tell ya, we're heading to the local pharmacy. Everything closes shop here 'round six in the evening, so they called the owner and he's going to open the place up so we can get you the last medicine you need."

He readjusts himself and looks back to the road.

The pills! I take them from my pocket and shove them to the front seat.

"Can you tell me what these are? The nurse couldn't really understand what I needed. Are they antibiotics?"

He examines the spray bottle. "This is used to clear out your nasal passage." He grabs the white pill box and lets out a hearty laugh. "Antibiotics? Nah kid, but you scored some excellent painkillers. If you don't want 'em, I'd gladly take 'em off your hands."

Even with my plugged ears I can still hear his heavy voice. My shoulders sink. Painkillers. Great. Just great. Painkillers weren't going to fix the problem; they were band aid medications like Adderall was. They didn't fix the real problem.

I take back the medications and slump into the cushions.

The moon outside is smothered in clouds when we near the pharmacy. A sly light emanates from the very back of the store. We wait a few minutes and listen to the taxi cab rumble in neutral. The light in the building flickers off and a tiny man steps out, locks the front door, and rushes to our cab.

The taxi man rolls the window down and the two men exchange dialogue that is too low for my ears to hear. The tiny man hands the taxi man a white bag, waves to the back seat, and takes off into the night.

Taxi man hands the bag back to me. Inside is a drip bottle for my ears.

"With all those things, you're going to be knocked out your entire stay here. Watch yourself, kid." His belly rumbles as he drives us back to the hostel free of charge.

Chapter 10

An Old Friend Returns

I try to decipher, again, the medication instructions. I still can't. The nurse said two, but from my previous experience with Adderall, I know my body has a high tolerance for pills. I drip the liquid from the pharmacy bottle into my ear and feel it slug its way down.

I've now dropped way below sea level.

I sure hope this works.

I roll the white pill in my hand.

Just a few weeks ago, I was addicted to another pill; a pill that soon became my daily, invisible crutch. I know my weaknesses well. I know I have an addictive personality and willpower alone does little to nothing to prevent it.

I stare at the pill.

I won't let it happen though. Not this time. The minute I'm better, there will be no more pills.

I dry swallow two.

I lie in bed and my head throbs, my ears crack and pop like a campfire.

I take another pill.

And wait.

The wall hits me. Hard and fast. One second, the pain continues, and the next, I'm comfortable. The energizer battery in me has been removed. My heartbeat is slowing. My eyelids droop.

And my ears? Do they hurt anymore? Who cares!

I feel fucking fantastic!

I roll another pill in my palms. Another can't hurt. I really do need them.

It feels good going down.

I'm asleep almost the second it wiggles down my throat.

⸗

When I wake up the next day, my symptoms are back and I feel worse then ever. I take four pills immediately.

The day blurs by.

I walk the town like a ghost.

A fish is said to have a three-second memory. I might have less than two seconds right now.

I sit for hours on a park bench and stare off into the mountains, wishing I could live here in a small cabin and write all day.

I laugh at how foolish I was to get addicted to a methamphetamine like Adderall. Why in God's name did I want to be that nervous and jumpy all the time? How could I stand being so—

So—

Awake all time? What the hell was I thinking?

Painkillers.

That slow-down sensation.

Carefree.

Now that … that was the way to go.

⸗

When we leave Switzerland the next day, we head to Italy. There, in a small convenience shop at the train station, is where I find a whole shelf of American antibiotics. I buy two without a prescription and am better within days.

But I keep the painkillers, just in case.

Chapter 11

The First of Many

I've never been drunk in my life.

Maybe I had a few extra gulps of wine when Mom and I volunteered to help with Communion at church here and there, but other than that, I was a saint when it came to alcohol.

And now, here I am, stumbling into Jordan, as I make my way from a desolate terminal to the train station lobby.

"Where, uh, where are we?" My words come out with a difficulty I'm not used to. I let out a short laugh that makes Dad shake his head. Either he's angry at me for being drunk, or we're lost.

I'm betting on both.

"Where—" I burp and the Norwegian alcohol burns its way up my throat. "Where are we, guys?"

The world is shifting back and forth, and by the time I know it, we are already in the empty lobby. I collapse to the floor and lean on a cement wall.

"Somewhere in Denmark," Dad replies. His eyes are racing so fast across the map in his hands, I feel dizzy just looking at them. I keep my head trained toward the ground.

Was it just one glass? No, it couldn't have been. I had Jordan's too. Did I take up the friendly Norwegian's offer for a third drink?

Hell! Who knows anymore?

Our final stretch back to Amsterdam after our month-long European tour was getting the best of us.

What a horrible place to start drinking.

The exchange rate was so horrendous, thanks to the recent U.S. deployment in Iraq, that we didn't even have enough money to buy food the last few days. Our rail passes and backpacks were all we had left. After leaving Switzerland, we traveled all around Europe. We stayed a few nights in various *Godfather*-esque Italian villages and made our way north to Berlin and Budapest.

The days had seemed short, and after Switzerland, the rest of the trip went on without a hitch. Mom was doing well and I was taking care not to take too many pills. My last addiction served as a good reminder of what I didn't want to become.

Tonight we started on our way back to Amsterdam to fly out the day after tomorrow. Problem was, we took the wrong train and had no idea where the hell we were.

A day-and-a-half empty stomach doesn't mix well with a hundred-and-ten-something-proof European alcohol. Especially if it's your first drink. Well, drinks that is.

"The exchange rate. That's what killed us," I mumble. Mom glances over from a wall bench that she had begun to unload her backpack on. I must sound ridiculous.

After their team huddle, Dad and Jordan walk toward me.

"Well," Dad begins, his voice tired, "we don't have a place to stay tonight and frankly, I haven't the faintest idea where we are exactly. But come tomorrow we can hitch a rail back to Amsterdam. We're only a half-day away or so. We should make the flight."

I bury my head in my hands.

Should?

My back slides down the concrete wall supporting me until I'm sprawled out on the floor.

European architecture is beautiful, and everything seems coated in some form of marble or another. The train station floor is no different.

It is made of a gorgeous green marble. But as of this moment, it feels as though it's the hardest and coldest surface known to man.

By the time I look up again, everyone is already unpacking and setting up camp for the night. They make pitiful makeshift pillows out of clothes.

I let my eyes drift across the station.

I have to go the bathroom. Bad.

It takes as much concentration as I can muster, and a few tumbles into the wall, before I'm able to hoist myself up to stand.

I hear giggling coming from the corner of the lobby as I make my way toward the bathroom. I turn and almost fall over.

So we aren't the only ones.

Two old women sit huddled together, bundled up, and physically built in such a way it looks like two bison waiting for a train.

I almost laugh aloud. My analogies were never the best, and now that I am drunk, they definitely aren't any better.

They both stop and look away in one smooth movement.

I turn and continue. I get to the men's bathroom door before realizing what my clouded mind has forgotten.

"Damn European bathrooms make you pay to use—" I curse under my breath. One of the women chuckles under a covering hand. My drunkenness is probably no secret.

I dig through my pockets knowing I'll find nothing.

I stumble over to the two women. They stiffen as I near.

"Hi!" I say as cheerfully as I can.

The two give curt smiles and nod. It's scary how synchronized one is with the other.

"Could I—" My body begins to waver as I move my hands into signs I had learned in American Sign Language class in high school last year. "Could I by chance borrow some Euro for the bathroom?"

I stop signing.

Nick, you're drunk. They don't speak English, so they definitely can't read sign language.

I laugh at the voice of reason in my head.

I make a round circle with my index finger that I fumble into a box shape. "Money." I point to the men's bathroom. "Bathroom."

Me Tarzan. You Jane.

The woman on the right looks somewhat annoyed with me. She digs her mittened hand into her body of fur and produces two Euro coins.

They drop into my open hands.

"Thank you. Thank you so much." I begin to bow, but lose my balance. I turn quickly to the bathroom before embarrassing myself further.

After I get back, everyone has long since fallen asleep, or are at least attempting to. I climb into a kitty-cat window sill by Jordan. It's still burning cold, but at least it isn't the dirty floor. I take some shirts from my bag and crush them together for a pillow. I take to an awkward fetal-like position since the window sill is almost half as long as my body.

I close my eyes and feel my body spin.

I'll never drink again.

I'm out for the night.

Chapter 12

The Long Plane Ride Home

The next day we make it to Amsterdam and grab the cheapest hostel we can find.

The next morning, the day of our flight, I wake up to crying.

Dad's bed is made. Jordan's bed is a wreck and Mom's bed looks untouched. I lean over my bunk bed and peer to the table in the middle of the small hostel room.

There she is. Hands buried in her face, her body lightly vibrating. She's Van Gogh.

No wonder I love that drawing of his. She is *At Eternity's Gate*.

I hop down the ladder and put my arms around and kneel next to her face.

"Mom?"

She looks up.

It's my dream all over again. The same ruined face. But this isn't my dream anymore. This is all too real.

"I want to die, Nick." She collapses into tears. When she's this low, her filters are gone. She's says anything that's on her mind, no matter what they sound like.

I hold tighter.

"I'm here, Mom. I love you and I'm here."

"It's so bad, so bad," she mumbles. "I can't live like this. I can't be like I was before. Oh God, I'm scared to go back!" She almost screams the word God.

Her head falls onto my shoulder. I run my hand across her hair.

"It'll be okay. We'll make it though this, alright?"

My eyes are watery.

Don't cry, Nick. Don't show weakness. Not now. You have to stay strong for her.

I suck it up.

We stay like this for a few minutes before her crying dies down.

"Go get some breakfast," she says.

I stand up and take a seat across from her. "Mom, I'm—"

"Please, just go. I'm okay."

I shake my head. She's a horrible liar.

"Nick—"

"I'm staying here."

"Go." I still hear the mother in her voice. "I'm fine. Alright? Please. Just go get some food."

I watch her for some time before getting up. I hug her and leave.

In the hallway, I collapse into a wall. I fumble in my pocket and toss a white pill into my mouth.

I hear crying again.

Close your eyes, Nick. Breathe.

What if she's right? What if it is back?

I pop another pill for good measure and head downstairs for breakfast. I wish I had a drink to couple with it.

Thank God I at least have pills.

⌒

Our plane, for some reason or another, is full. They offer us the chance to stay another night at a nearby hotel in the heart of Amsterdam. All expenses paid, and we'd get a refund on our flight tickets.

Jordan can't stay another day, but Dad thinks we should consider it. So does Mom.

"This is a trip of a lifetime," she says. "And we shouldn't go home early just on account of me."

I don't buy her lie. I know she's doing horribly.

I refuse to stay another night.

We get booked for the next available flight.

～

Mom cries the whole way home.

I whisper anything I can think of to keep her positive so she doesn't fully break down. The passengers around us kindly put in their earplugs to drown us out.

She doesn't sleep and neither do I.

Fourteen hours later, we arrive in Seattle. Our family friend, Jim, is there to pick us up.

The family crashes when we get home.

I lie in my bed for a few hours.

Back home.

The European dream is done. Back to reality. Back to another year of school. Back to trying to figure out how the hell I am going to figure out my future. Back to struggling to figure out how to force myself to write. Back home to a sick mother.

Vacations sure are nice. But when you get home, the same problems are there.

I left with an addiction.

I take all the remaining pills I have to get to sleep.

And now, I'm back with another addiction.

That night, I don't have a single dream.

Not even one.

Chapter 13

A Child's Dream is Still a Dream (November 2003)

When Bob Barker walks out onto the stage of *The Price Is Right*, I jump out of my seat and clap like a monkey on speed and scream like a girl at a rock concert.

It's only been a few months since coming back from Europe, and the rollercoaster of my life has yet to slow down.

I look over to Duff. Well, Kyle actually, but everyone calls him Duff. He's been my friend since junior high. I shake him and he does the same to me. His eyes are wide like an alien. Or like a kid who just got his first glimpse of Santa.

Our birthdays were only a few days apart from each other and we always laughed about how much we wanted to go to a taping of *The Price Is Right* when we were kids. We made a promise to make a trek down to California when we both turned eighteen.

We laughed at how silly it seemed back then. We'd never go through with it.

And now, Bob Barker is in the same room as us.

The stage he is on is much smaller than it appears on television. The audience, with the modern tricks of cinematography, is also made to look larger than it actually is.

The crowd roars as the announcer calls the first five people out of audience.

Duff's football frame bounces around like he's doing a warm-up routine.

I continue my girlish scream.

This, as dumb as it sounds, is what dreams are made of.

I put more thought into this than I did colleges for next year. My advisors at school think I'm crazy. But to me, this trip signifies that I can complete any dream, no matter who laughs it down. It just takes perseverance.

The game continues and I watch in a trance.

And suddenly, halfway through, something happens that is indescribable.

"Look out folks, here comes," the announcer's voice feels as though the loudspeakers are directly above my head. "Nicholas Rogennnnnn! Come on down, you're the next contestant on *The Price Is Right*!"

My heart stops.

⌒

Duff and I had gotten in line for the taping before sunrise. Long before sunrise, in fact, and already there was a line trailing around the gates of the CBS headquarters.

When we got in line, we busied ourselves by talking to the "veterans" of the show, such as the old women who came here daily, sitting in front row seats for years trying to get on. We discussed the logistics and secrets behind Plinko, arguably the best game on the show.

After hours of waiting, they let us inside the gates and we were forced through yet another large line. By now, our excitement was boiling over.

Every person in line was considered to be a potential contestant on air, so they sent us through an interview with a panel of three, scribble-happy judges.

"You have thirty seconds. Tell us why you're here."

That's all you had. Thirty seconds to make three judges you'd never met like you.

"I'm skipping school," I said. "Saved up all my lunch money for this moment."

I told them it was my dream. A dumb dream, but a dream nonetheless.

They smiled and scribbled away on their clipboard. They smiled me on and Duff went through the gauntlet with the same answers. Neither of us had the slightest expectation to get our name called out.

That is, until they actually did call my name.

Chapter 14

The Price Is Right

I look over at a wide-eyed Duff mouthing the words, "Oh my God." For a split second, I swear my heart is never going to start back up again. I leap up from my seat and start high-fiving everyone around me. Their screaming drowns out the cheesy overhead music I'd listened to since I was a kid.

Oh my God!

I jog down the aisle and run past the other contestants standing on Contestants' Row. I get to the last spot and look up at the small and colorful stage, and there is Bob Barker. Standing right in front of me!

My mind is moving so fast I can't keep a clear thought.

"Young Nicholas has joined us," Bob says as his small body gestures toward me. He spins around and points at a large curtain behind him. "And will you look at what my beauties are bringing out here for you to bid on!"

Two women, dressed all in red, appear. They are gorgeous, but my attention on them doesn't last for more than a second.

Rod Roddy, the famous colorfully dressed announcer who'd been on the show since 1986, had recently died from cancer and the replacement had yet to live up to his shine. His voice took time to make the audience stop screaming as he went into a spiel about the cookware that the two women were trying to show off with their best impression of Vanna White.

Bob sends his attention to me. "How about a bid, Nicholas?"

"$650." I do a goofy grin and try to remain as calm as I can.

This can't be happening.

"His bid is $650!" Bob says as he goes down the line of other contestants to collect their bids.

I look back to Duff who gives me a thumbs up.

I did it. I always said I would do this, and I believed in myself, and I did it. I got on.

"Actual retail price," Bob interrupts my thoughts, "$850! Winner, Donnnnnaa!" He stretches out her name for effect. I clap like mad. The woman on the end leaps into the air toward Bob. I'm surprised her hug doesn't crush poor Bob's tiny body.

Everyone on Contestants' Row takes a seat on the special chairs behind the podiums. As I sit down, I feel a barrage of hands shake my shoulder as people near the front congratulate me.

After the commercial break, we all hop back to our podiums as the announcer calls another player down. Cynthia, a short Hispanic woman, bounds down the aisle and rips past me.

Bob laughs. "Cynthia? Where are you going? Cynthia! Back here!" The woman turns around and runs to the other end of the long podium where she was originally supposed to stop.

"I thought she looked like such a nice lady, then immediately she tried to take Nicholas's place away from him over there," Bob says with his usual cheer.

I almost pass out. This is too much, too fast.

Bob whips around again toward the curtains.

"What are we going to bid on, fellers?"

The curtains are thrown aside and out comes one of the Vanna White impersonators. She waves her arm around a large refrigerator.

I turn to Duff for advice and he shrugs as Cynthia places her bid.

"Nicholas, you're the bidder."

All eyes focus on me. I look to the ground and try my best to collect my thoughts. With the roaring audience though, my brain is a pile of mush.

"$1,150."

I sigh and look back. *Way too much.* I shake my head at Duff.

The next couple moments waiting for Bob to collect everyone's bid feels like an eternity. I strain by head so I can hear Bob's voice through the screeching audience.

"Actual retail price—" He pauses as he looks toward the card in his hand.

And the award goes to—

"$1,179! Winner, Nicholasss!"

This time, I'm sure I'm going to pass out. I throw my hands in the air and make my way to the side of the stage. A woman behind the cameras with a clipboard and a mic on her ear motions wildly for me to follow her up some stairs. I hurry toward her and make my way to Bob's side.

My heart starts up again. *Isn't this a symptom of a heart attack?*

"Right over here, Nicholas." I shake Bob's hand but want to hug him. He leans toward me and shouts, "And we're not wasting any time! Show him the loot!"

I turn my attention to the stage where an entertainment system rolls out.

With the cameras no longer focused on us, Bob begins to chat with me. My attention on the prize completely wavers.

"Where you from?"

"I, uh—" I suddenly know what the expression "cat got your tongue?" means. "I'm from the Seattle area."

"Very nice."

"It's my birthday," I blurt out.

"So I hear." He laughs.

I must look like an idiot.

The announcer's voice fades into the sound of the entire audience clapping. The camera rotates back to us.

Everything is moving faster than I can comprehend.

"Nicholas just became eighteen years old, and he's about to become a winner on *The Price Is Right!*"

Beside me is the game I remember watching countless times with Mom during the days when I skipped school just to watch the show. Squeeze Play. It's the easiest game they have.

Bob begins explaining. "You'll win that prize if you remove the right number." He points to the different numbers. "Now this three … that's the first number in the price. This eight is the last number in the prize. Of the middle numbers, do you want me to take out the one, the nine, or the three?" The microphone he's holding moves to my face.

The audience roars with answers.

Oh shit! I was too busy talking with Bob to notice what the prize was.

I try to think fast, but my mind is a blender on high. I look to Duff for an answer. He shouts out the number three and waves his answer in the air.

No—

Time is frozen.

I can do this by myself. I do everything by myself. I can do this.

"The nine," I say, confident that I, and the audience, are correct and Duff is wrong.

"The nine goes! And it squeezes together to $3,138 dollars. We want a winner!"

The silence is unbearable.

The echo of the "wah-wah" sound makes the crowd perform a universal sigh.

Bob looks to me with a frown. "Ahh. Too bad! Happy Birthday anyway."

I shake his hand and look over to the camera to see the woman with the clipboard waving at me again to follow her. I tag along with her off-stage to a set of seats in the corner of the audience.

She smiles. "Congratulations on winning the fridge. I just need you to fill out some paperwork."

"Okay," I say.

I sit next to Donna, the one I thought would certainly hug Bob to death. Her face is lit like she took a hit of speed between commercial breaks. "I can't believe you won! Are you excited? How was it? Was it fun? What are you going to do with a fridge? Do you live with your parents? I mean … what are they going to say?" I almost can't process her run-on sentences and fill out the paperwork at the same time.

"Thanks."

"Is it really your birthday?" she finally asks a single, answerable question.

I laugh. "Yeah, it is. It's been a dream of my friend and mine to come and see the show since we were kids. So we made a promise to come here when we both turned eighteen, and—"

"And you actually got on!" She throws her hands up in cheer. "That's sooooo exciting!"

"I know. It's so crazy that this is even happening. I mean, I've always dreamed of this, but I never thought I'd actually go through with it. Let alone get this far."

"Dreams are a funny thing. Because if you go for it, there's nothing that can stop you—Oh my God!" She points to the stage.

Cynthia, the small Hispanic woman, is literally collapsing on stage. She has just won a car.

Donna and I stand up and applaud. She hugs me and I suddenly feel just as cheerful as her, even after losing the entertainment system.

Dreams are a funny thing indeed.

⌒

I spin the Big Wheel, go well over a hundred, and am eliminated from the show. Depressing as it may seem to not go on to the Showcase Showdown, I'm so high from just being on the show, that I don't feel the least bit disappointed. After the taping, I follow the rest of the winners to a back room where we fill out more paperwork and pay the taxes that each of our prizes require. On our way out we're handed signed pictures of Bob.

Duff almost tackles me as I leave the room. His smile is wider than I'd ever seen.

"Damn nine," I say, and we laugh all the way to our hotel room across the street.

Chapter 15

Back to Reality (December 2003)

I try to walk down the hallway toward my room, but lose balance and direction and slam into the wall. My shoulder crunches beneath my weight.

The world spins. *What the hell am I doing?*

I close my eyes, hoping it will help steady my vision.

I attempt to throw my weight off the wall, but fail. I slam back into the wall and slide to the ground, resting my back on the wall.

I examine the wine bottle in my hands.

Am I really trying to kill myself?

Of course, I know I'm not, but it's still a valid question.

Mom's been gone for almost three days now. Dad and I haven't bothered to call the police or anything. We know where she is.

Since Amsterdam last summer, Mom had been better. No relapses. No hospital visits. Our family, for the first time, was normal in that respect. But mental illnesses were an odd thing. They never really went away and they certainly weren't in the least bit predictable. Over the few months since getting back, Mom had slowly become addicted to gambling in her, now abundant, free time. Now that she was no longer in a hospital or in her bed, she was working again, and had plenty of time for hobbies.

Gambling was now her hobby.

She never touched the tables. Just the slots. The lights and sounds were like a circus to her head, lighting off as many neurons as her manic mood swings could intake. Most of my life, I had learned to play my cards with the depression side of her. When it came to her manic state, I usually folded.

We've shut off as many credit cards as we can. It's just a matter of time now.

Back when I was a kid, she'd go on massive shopping sprees on her manic highs. Ever see someone spend an entire day shopping at a Goodwill? Seven or eight hours? That was my Mom.

And now she's traded addictions.

Just like I have. Adderall for painkillers and alcohol.

Thank you, Europe!

Almost every night since coming back, I've sneaked into Mom's medicine cabinet; a jungle of pills for every occasion and mood. I usually choose a pill called Clorazapam. I researched it online and decided it was close enough to what I had in Europe.

It's like legal chloroform. It literally erases your brain.

Amazing how something so horrible can be so wonderful. So freeing. It makes every problem you've ever had seem pitiful.

I can't remember how many I took. Three? Maybe four?

However many I took, it's still not making me feel any better.

Dammit, Mom! I'm sick of worrying. I'm sick of her spending our family's money.

Truthfully though, I'm sick of myself.

"Why am I doing this?" I ask the wine bottle I juggle between my hands. What happened? One second everything was alright, and the next I'm doing this to myself. Why, why, why?!?

God, I wish you would answer me. For once.

I do it because I'm scared … and because I can't stop myself. I don't know if there really is a "why" to it. Maybe I'm just destined to be a failure. Living that Van Gogh quote I scribbled down in Amsterdam. That's the only explanation I can give myself.

I hoist myself back up and take baby steps across the hallway.

My door to my room bursts open as I smash through it. The bed is a comfortable crash.

Luckily, Dad can sleep through an air raid.

I can't ever let him see me like this.

I take out my swivel corkscrew and take off the cork. I gulp down a mouthful of light wine.

I look around my room.

It all makes sense. I'm a loser who's good at hiding it.

No girlfriend. No college plans. No anything. School is winding down and I have no idea what I am going to do after that.

I crack open the closet and pull out a dusty shoe box. Inside, I dig through the stacks of stories I used to write as a kid.

And my writer's dream? What the hell happened to that?

The one thing in my life I am truly in love with. And I stopped writing in fear of failure.

What did someone like me have to write about? A fridge I won on a game show? A sappy story about a kid with a crazy mother? What I wrote was all garbage. I was chasing a made-up dream that wasn't meant for me.

I throw the entire box into the wall and the contents of the box rain down like confetti.

I take another swig.

Pills and alcohol. Writers are supposed to be smart. Not so stupid that they risk their lives like I am doing.

Hemingway would be proud.

I close my eyes right when the front door opens. Mom is finally home.

My eyes pop back open. I grab the wall and pull myself up.

She can't see my like this.

Not like this! I'm a fucking wreck!

I throw the bottle to the ground and it bleeds into the carpet like cat piss. I rush to the bathroom where the automatic lights send my eyes wincing. Brush back the hair. Soak the skin around the eyes with warm water. Being high on pills and drunk on cheap wine doesn't go away quickly.

I take a large sigh.

A fog is creeping through every crevice in my brain.

I'm so angry I could scream, but the moment I step into the living room, every ounce of resentment disappears.

Her hair, blonde and frizzled, is grossly unkempt. Her eyelids are droopy and she reeks of cigarettes. But there's not a single tear in her ear. She looks as angry as I felt earlier.

I sit in the chair across from her in our living room. I hold my head up so I don't topple over. I wait for her to talk first. I'm afraid I will slur my words. I can't look weak. I can't be this way. Not now.

We can't both be a wreck, or else who's going to be the one to lean on?

She stares at the centerpiece on the table for some time before she speaks in a whisper.

"At work, I get so excited at my job. The kids just get me so worked up. And so—" She pauses. "Maybe it's the colors. The noise. I don't even play the tables. I have no interest in those. Only the slots. It's not even about the money. I don't understand what the lure is."

She meets my eyes.

I gulp and talk slowly. "Mom, it's—"

"It's not okay. I don't know how to stop. This addiction … I can't just will it away. I've tried. So help me God, I've tried."

I sigh. She's stealing my line.

Mother and son, both addicted.

How cute.

"You want to know … what I think." I rub my eyes, yawn, and try to play off my slow speech as being tired.

"I think you work so hard for others, but never think of yourself.

You slave away at work. Slave away organizing these support groups of yours. But when do you ever have time for yourself?"

She grins. A sad one, but a grin nonetheless.

"How'd you get so smart at your age?"

I smile too. I'm always ready with advice for others, just never for myself.

"I may be a codependent, but," she laughs, "so are you, Nick."

"Me? Right." I roll my eyes.

"You are the one who pushed me through all those dark years. Crawled into bed after Dad went to work so you could make sure I was alright. You always came home straight away after school. So tell me, when did you ever have time for yourself?"

I often forget Mom has a double major in psychology and education, so she is an expert at reversing questions on others.

Like mother like son.

Maybe that is the reason I am so fucked up.

I sigh. "We're getting off track. Mom, give me your purse."

She doesn't argue and hands over a small purse. I cruise through her stack of cards. The words are moving on the cards. It takes several minutes before I'm able to pull out all the dangerous ones.

Bank of America? Check.

BECU? Check.

I hand back her purse.

She smiles. "How did I get blessed with such a great son." It's not a question.

"Mom—" I stop in mid-sentence.

Dad walks into the living room, naked except for the white underwear he stole from me since he didn't have a clean pair. His tiny, bulky frame stops. He looks over to where we sit.

His eyes flutter over to Mom for less than a blink.

He says nothing, but we hear everything.

He continues to the kitchen. Mom is quiet, her head bowed down.

Guilt is sitting with her. Correction: sitting with us.

Dad leaves with a cup of water in his hands. He doesn't look Mom's way again.

We're alone again.

"I know what you're going through," I blurt out. I almost slap myself for saying it. The knight in his white armor reveals his chinks.

Mom lifts her head. "You do?"

I get up and waver in my stand. "I do." I don't try to elaborate. I've said too much already.

I turn to walk away but stop.

"Mom, I love you," I say, my back still turned to her. My eyes can no longer stay open. "I'm not disappointed in you. And I'm here for you. Next time you feel the urge, call me. I won't yell. I won't be mad. But please know you're not alone. You need help and your family is here. I'm here."

What a codependent at heart.

Why can't I follow my own advice?

I keep walking and don't turn back. Mom got the point, I'm sure. I stumble into my room and crawl into the corner.

I pick up the wine bottle and take a gulp of whatever is left.

I make a quick prayer for God to watch over Mom and help her. I promise Him I'll stay by her side.

I crawl to my bed, but don't even make it there before I'm fast asleep.

Chapter 16

A Writer in Waiting (April 2004)

I hold my fist mid-motion before it comes down on the heavy wooden door. I read the fancy gold lettering plated at eye level with me. "Mr. Brown. Sumner High School Guidance Counselor." I turn toward the receptionist who has waved me in.

"Don't worry, you can knock." The receptionist is soft, winding down after a day full of excuses, angry teenagers, and everything else high school kids throw at her. "He's expecting you."

But he's not expecting what I have to say.

"Thank you." I twist back to the door and let my hand finish the motion. My bony hand knocks lightly on the wood. The door bursts open. Mr. Brown's quarterback body rises above me like something out of a horror movie. I look over to his desk, where a half-eaten sandwich and its wrapping sprawl out. I wipe the sweat from my forehead with my sleeve.

He extends his massive arm.

"Come on in, Nick." I shake his hand and feel my own crack under his grip, my bones conforming into an awkward half-moon shape. "I was just finishing up my lunch here."

He motions to a chair in front of his desk much like a psychologist does to a patient. He sinks into his office chair and tucks the sandwich away.

"Sorry, Mr. Brown." I feel guilty for interrupting his lunch. "I just

66

got out of class and thought I could come a few minutes earlier than I was scheduled. I didn't mean to—"

"No, no. It's perfectly okay. Lunch can always wait." He grins. "How about we get down to business?"

I gulp. I'd probably only spoken to a guidance counselor of any sort once or twice in my life, but I already know what this is going to be about. Mr. Brown seems like a likeable man, even if his old football status from his high school days is plastered all over his room. It is creepy in a way.

"Sure," I say.

He takes out a file from underneath his pile of papers, opens it, and begins scrolling through it. His broad shoulders hover over my transcripts.

"Three point nine grade average. Honor roll. Leadership—" He trails off as he looks up, smiling with his relaxed brown eyes.

My face is turning red. I try to reply, but instead just nod my head.

"Let me be blunt. You are a fantastic student, Nick. There's no doubt about that." Again, he lets his words die off.

I wonder where the "but" is going to come into play.

He takes another page from the file and sets it on top. From where I'm sitting, I can't tell what it is.

"This is from your Advisory classes." He sighs, loud enough to make it feel like a breathing exercise he teaches during football practices. "That's why I had you come. You're graduating here in a couple months and … and I want to hear what your plans are for continuing your education after high school. As far as I can see, you left most of these worksheets empty."

I swallow hard. I hate this question. Why is it so hard to tell people that I don't really know what I want to do with my life? And why is the world so narrow to think a kid would know what they want to be doing twenty years down the road? How do I tell him what I mess I had become? How do I tell him that I want to be a writer but don't know where to start?

Over the past few months, I've thought about my situation. The secret hole I have buried myself in. The only solution I see is to dig myself out. But my shovel isn't in a college, I know that much.

"I've decided to take a year off before going to college."

"Have you applied anywhere?" he asks, as though he doesn't hear my response.

"No." My answer makes him wince.

He looks confused, his eyebrows arching in odd directions. "With grades like this, you can pretty much go anywhere you want. The sky is the limit for someone like you."

Now it is my turn to sigh. I try to make it as loud as his was.

"My Dad took a year off after high school and went to Africa. He helped build houses, transport things, all that. He says it was the most eye-opening experience he's ever had."

"And is that what you're going to do?"

"Well, no." I look away. I have no idea what I'm going to do. "But I've decided to take a year off anyway, and do something like he did. That way I can figure out just what it is I want to do with my life. I'm in no rush to find out. I don't want to bury myself in debts until I'm forty just because I feel like there is a time limit to go to school." I shrug.

It isn't like I am lying, but it sure as hell feels like it.

My words don't seem to soak into him. He must have met hundreds of kids just like me. "But that's what community college is for. Why not figure it out while you're going?"

His answers feel pushy. *And, what, Mr. Brown? End up becoming a guidance counselor in a high school? Like you did?*

"Like I said, I don't want to rush through my life. I want to figure out my direction before I take off running."

Mr. Brown leans back in his chair and folds his hands behind his head. It's the pre-game stretch before taking out his wild card.

"And after this year of hiatus, you'll go back to school?" he asks.

"Definitely." To be honest, I want to go to college. After everything else fits together that is. Why wait for my inspiration to write to come to me? Why can't I make my own adventures worth writing about while I am still young and not tied down to anything?

My logic makes sense to me.

"Do you know the statistics of high school graduates that actually go back and finish their education after they take a break immediately following high school?"

"No," I admit.

"It's low. Real low."

He's silent for a moment, trying to let his play soak in.

"Mr. Brown." I look him in the eyes. "I'm not most people. The reason I have those grades in the first place isn't because I'm all that smart. It's because I try my best at everything I do."

He nods. "I know, I know."

Instead of a rebuttal, he agrees with me. I'm surprised. He sighs again and leans forward. He crosses his arms on his desk.

"You're the kind of kid who can say that and I truly believe they will."

His words suddenly give me the urge to scream, to yell for help, to tell him that I'm living a lie. That I'm living so dangerously, that I feel my life is spinning out of control. I want to cry and ask for help. For advice. To find out the answer to why I am destroying myself. I want to ask him why I'm so goddamn secret about my life. I can help everyone else, but I can't help myself.

But I don't scream. I simply say, "thank you," like I always do.

His eyebrows lift and a sadness develops in his voice that I haven't heard through his earlier pep talk. "Just be careful Nick, okay? You're going to be going places and I sure as hell don't want to see you fall through the cracks."

"I won't." I get up from the seat and head for the door. I can't stay and lie any more. I have to get away.

"And I hope you find your direction in the next year."

I turn before heading out the door. "I will."

But I know I won't.

Chapter 17

Graduation (June 2004)

I shut my bedroom door tight before stumbling toward my closet. My head is starting to swirl as I trip on a small pile of clothes in the middle of my room. The small misstep sends my body barreling toward the ground. Luckily, the wall catches me.

I'm surprised the walls don't have dents from how many times I've fallen into them lately.

I hear my shoulder blade snap.

Why do I keep doing this to myself?

"Are you okay?" Mom calls out from the living room.

"I'm fine," I yell as I try my best not to stumble over my words like I did my feet.

The Clorazapam is starting to take effect; half an hour earlier than I expected. Though I should have known it would when I downed over half a handful of the antipsychotic drug.

I lift myself back up from the wall, cursing under my breath for being stupid enough to take so many pills on such an important day.

I had grown immune to smaller doses over the last few months, but this time I knew I had taken one too many. It had started out recreationally. I had used the pills to escape the feeling that I was going nowhere in my life. And now, it had become my only reality, a daily medication I used to make it through the day.

I laugh. It feels forced, but it's still a laugh. "Oh, the irony of it all."

I take off for the closet again, and upon reaching the fold-out double doors plastered with teenage memorabilia, I open them and take a seat on the ground. My hands fumble in a messy pile of clothing stuffed in the corner. After what seems like minutes of digging, my hands feel the glass of the wine bottle I had stowed earlier in the week. I gently take it from my closet and let it roll in my hands for a moment before removing the corkscrew from my pocket.

I begin unscrewing until it is just about to pop open. I stop and shut my eyes, the blackness behind my eyelids swirls with sporadic colors not unlike the ones seen after a straight flash from a camera. I try my best to focus. I can faintly hear my grandparents talking in the kitchen.

Good.

I pop the cork. The blast sends my eyelids open. My hand instinctively braces my body on the closet door, as if knowing I would tip over otherwise. I reach back in the clothing pile and produce a large milk glass. I fill it to the brim with wine. The Clorazapam has dulled my senses, but I can still smell the acidic flavor of the dark red wine. It gurgles out like a river.

I take a quick shot. My face twitches. I hold back the urge to puke it up.

Oh God!

My eyes leak out a stream of tears.

I take another shot before I'm too disgusted to take another.

No wonder wine isn't for shot gunning!

Before I know it, the glass is empty.

As I take my time on the second glass, I can feel my stomach in an uproar with the sudden intake of fluid. When I move, it's as though my stomach is a fish bowl; the water swishing back and forth like a storm.

I feel dizzy now. Putting the empty glass down, I can't imagine how I am going to pull this off. I leave the glass and bottle on top of the clothes and rise to my feet, feeling like a baby attempting to stand for the first time. I close the closet door and rest my head on it.

"Nick?" My family is ready at the front door. "You ready? The ceremony starts in an hour."

I bend back my head until I feel stable, or as stable as I can be. In front of me, taped to the closet door, are my grades from last quarter. I had been so proud of them. All three point nines and four pointers. I turn away from them and look to the corner of my bed. My graduation cap and gown lay neatly there, both still in the plastic I had bought them in.

I sigh and head out my door.

The gown and cap blur out of view.

I'm not going to need them.

Not today.

⌒

"You know, Nick," Grandma says as she hugs me from the side. "You never actually told your Grandpa and me why you're not down there."

I close my eyes and groan. If I wasn't so drunk and doped up on pills, I probably would have never answered her. I would have been too embarrassed of myself. Now though, I couldn't care less. When I reopen my eyes, my head bobbles. My vision blurs the crowd of screaming families as though the whole stadium is a boat crashing through rocky current.

I turn to Grandma. I can only make out her outline since my head is spinning too uncontrollably to make out any of her defined, wrinkled features.

"I lied on my senior project." My words come out perfectly. Over the years I have mastered the art of pretending to be something I'm not. And right now, I am pretending that I'm not just another drug-addicted kid.

"Why?" she asks.

I turn away from her and watch as my graduating class on the field below commences their ceremony without me; a sea of purple gowns moving this way and that. I close my eyes again. The view is too far way and the loudspeakers are too crappy to tell who is actually speaking.

How poetic. I'm still graduating, but banned from walking. Outcast. How fitting.

"Because … I didn't care anymore." Before she can answer, I rattle off the rehearsed response I tell everyone who asks me why I'm not living up to my potential. "Everyone but me seems to know what they want to do with their life. I feel like I'm the only one who just doesn't get it." I laugh and feel the wine gurgle up my throat. "I feel so pressured to know what I want to do by now. What college I want to go to. What profession I want to master. I got so tired of the pressure that I decided to give up, take a year off—"

Mr. Brown was right all along. I could have been anything I wanted. Could have even been a writer. If only I had just tried—

"That's what your father did. Went down to Africa." Grandma squeezes me even tighter. "It'll all come to you. You'll use those gifts God gave you sooner or later."

The class treasurer is now going full speed into his speech and everyone around us begins to holler and clap.

"That's the whole problem, Grandma. I don't know about that. I wanted to be a writer, but I hated everything I wrote. So I don't even bother trying anymore. And the problem is, I don't know why I can't. Write that is. I've always been good at it. I just can't seem to do it anymore." I try to wiggle my way out of her hug. Grandma hugs are impossible to escape from. "The only thing I actually put effort into was going to some stupid game show I loved as kid." I turn to her. "I mean, how sad is that? That I put more effort into a dumb dream I had when I was a kid than planning for my future?"

Grandma puts her hand on my face and a chill runs through me.

"Going to that show proved something, Nick." I feel her wrinkles move across my skin. "It proved you can do anything if you put your mind to it. It doesn't matter how dumb you think the dream was. You've missed the point."

She lets go of me and puts her index finger on my chest.

"You did it. You put your mind to it and did it. You followed your dream. That's what you need to realize. And that's no different than what you have to do now." She leans in to me. "What you need to do now is dream again."

I say nothing in return. I wonder if she notices that I'm on something, but a part of me knows that even if she did, it wouldn't make a difference.

As my name rolls by the presenter, my parents and grandparents stand up and cheer the loudest.

Chapter 18

Fourth of July (July 2004)

By the time Mike arrives with his Fourth of July beam plastered on his face, I am already well past being lightly drunk. He comes bouncing down the hill toward the lakefront with eyes lit like a ten-year-old boy itching to get his hands on some fireworks, when in all actuality he is twenty-three, only a few years older than me. I try to grin. Mike is my favorite cousin who never misses my family's Fourth of July parties.

Earlier that week, I found out my parents were looking to adopt.

Adopt. The word is bitter in my mouth.

I'm not the brother a little girl needs to look up to. I'm a mess.

But it's only talk, and I hope it stays that way.

As for now, I'm back into my usual groove. Drinking away my worries, and so far, it's working like a charm.

I turn away from Mike and continue watching the fireworks being shot out over the lake. I nurse my bottle of pop, a mix of Dr. Pepper and vodka. It tastes horrible, but it sure is doing the trick.

"Heya, Nicky!" I get up and bear hug his matching small frame. Aside from his shorter hair and bushy beard, we look like brothers.

"You ready?" It was tradition every year that I would wait until he drove up from Longview and we'd head out to the Indian reservation and pick up as many bags full of fireworks as we could fit into his trunk. On the way back, we'd stop by a gun shop, buy some gunpowder, then head to the Goodwill and buy anything we could blow into a million pieces.

And as our custom would have it, we'd spend the rest of the afternoon creating our own production line of illegal explosives. Of course, we had our mishaps over the years. Dad blowing his eardrums out two years ago with an oxyacetylene balloon. The hot-air balloon that didn't take right to the wind and lit our neighbor's roof on fire instead.

Safe to say, we now try to detour from balloons as much as possible.

"Earth to Nick. Well, we going or not?" Mike jabs me in the arm. His light push almost sends me to the ground.

"You okay, Nick?"

I smile. When Mom was sick in the hospital, I had mastered the art of faking. I was able to fool almost anyone into thinking I was okay. Being drunk, though slightly more difficult, is no different.

Pretending is my gift.

"Yeah, I'm cool." I massage my temples. "But I'm so broke this year."

"So?" He pushes me again and motions me to follow up the steps. "So what? I'll cover you. Come on!"

I shake my head. Everything is bleeding together as though I am riding a carousel.

"Nah … I can't. I think I'll just lay low this year."

"What?" His face scrunches up. Saying no is a knife to his stomach. "No way, man. You are not bailing."

I bite my tongue.

"Okay," I say as I hold back a burp. "Let's go."

His smile returns.

As we make our way to Mike's car, Dad joins us. He never seems to want to steer too far away from the action.

↜

A loud explosion wakes me from my sleep. Above me the tiny lights of a mortar blast litter the night sky, falling like confetti until eventually fading from view.

I stop breathing.

Where am I?

It takes a minute to gauge my surroundings and realize that I'm sitting behind the house in a lawn chair. Behind and above me are a dozen or so people gathered on our balcony looking out over the lake at the light show on the other island.

Oh my God. My face slams into my hands. *How long have I been out?*

I find a blanket wrapped around me, snug and tight.

I tear it off and stand up. My head spins and I fall right back into the chair. I look down the hill to our launching pad. It's empty. No kids around it. No sputtering fireworks, only a black void where something should have been. Our family shared the fireworks board with our neighbors, since both my mom and neighbor's mom were tired of all of us catching the lawn and plants on fire each year. With store-bought sparklers and homemade explosives attached to old Barbies and Mr. Potato Heads, the fireworks board was always the center of attention for everyone that came to our parties. Our two families were a good team.

Now the launching pad is empty and Mike is nowhere in sight. I try to remember what had happened, but I can't remember a thing. My head is pounding like a hammer with every firework that explodes in the air. Honestly, I can't even tell if I had ever even gotten to Mike's car. Frankly, I don't even know where he went.

I'm a mess.

And now the secret is out. I look to the blanket I had tossed aside. My parents must have found me, drunk and passed out. Instead of waking me, they wrapped me up in a blanket.

I rub my eyes. I'm an idiot to think they wouldn't have noticed me the last year. They've probably known all this time—

"Hey, Nick." A voice from the neighbor's porch to the right startles me. A small blond boy I don't recognize walks into the porch light.

How does he know my name?

"Why wasn't there any fireworks?"

"There is." I point across the lake.

"No," he laughs. "That's for old people! I mean why didn't you light off anything? Something big!" His eyes grow to saucer-size.

My stomach churns, and it isn't due to the alcohol.

"I"—my stutter can't be hidden—"I didn't really feel up to it this year."

The boy bows his head, but immediately pops it back up with a smile wider than anything I've ever seen.

"Remember that year you blew up that huge, life-sized Barbie doll with that mortar bomb you made out of gunpowder and a tennis ball and the pieces flew everywhere and everyone was on the ground laughing 'cause it was so funny?" The boy gasps for air after his excited sentence.

I don't know how to respond and choose to say nothing.

"And 'member that time when that friend of Mike's, Joe, went out on your Seadoo and he had this problem with his eyes—" The boy mimics Joe, his eyes rolling back and forth rapidly. "And so he didn't see the balloons you guys loaded with bombs that were supposed to explode in the air with the sparklers as fuses?"

Again with the balloons.

"Yeah—"

"But the sparklers you used for the fuse burst the balloons and fell on Joe and blew him straight off the Seadoo and everyone thought he was dead?!"

I can't help but chuckle. "Yeah, I remember that."

"That was so cool."

We laugh together until a blast from across the lake blows our voices away.

"I seriously wait every year to see what you're going to do next!"

Oh, please, stop already, kid.

"And this year—" His smile disappears as he wiggles his foot into the ground. "So what about next year?"

"I hope so."

He meets my eyes and smiles. "I hope so too! 'Night!"

He takes off into the darkness and disappears.

I hide my face in my hands.

Some mysterious kid who looks up to me. That's all I need.

"I'm a fucking mess, kid. You don't want to look up to me."

I begin to cry.

My mind shifts to the adoption rumor again. How can I be an older brother when I can't even take care of myself?

Next year, would I still be a wreck? Could I be looked up to again?

Yeah, kid, I hope so too.

I wrap myself in the thin blanket and watch the display of fireworks die out across the lake.

Chapter 19

The New Hire (September 2004)

The Pepsi headquarters in Tacoma sure as hell isn't how I had imagined it. When I went for my interview two weeks ago, it seemed so much more glamorous. The parking lot was smooth pavement, not chipped and riddled with tire-flattening holes. The large neon sign, which had been fully illuminated in the afternoon sun, was now dim and a few letters looked almost completely burnt out.

The surrounding neighborhood was different as well. It was the heart of industrial Tacoma, and far from being the glitzy place you'd think a major corporation would sink extra roots into. The air was a mixture of sweat and smokestacks, and the street Pepsi was on was marked with abandoned and rundown factories.

It had all seemed so glorious when I wanted a job here, but now that I had a position, I wasn't so sure.

I told Mr. Brown my year-long "sabbatical" would be full of adventures and intriguing locales. Not this.

Before I get out of my car, I take out the tiny blue pill in my pocket.

Adderall.

When I scrounged around my room for my old prescription earlier today, I told myself I wouldn't get hooked again. I just needed it this once, to help show my new employers that I am a nonstop hard worker.

Just one. That's it.

I swallow the pill and hope that I'm not lying to myself.

The door beeps as I enter the small lobby. I walk up to the front desk that is shielded by a cheap pane of plastic. It reminds me of quarantine in some disaster movie. Protect everyone from the outside virus. Or maybe, just maybe, it is the other way around.

I ring the bell and a middle-aged woman appears and smiles. Not a "how can I help you" smile, but a real one.

Maybe this isn't going to be so bad.

"Hi, I'm Nick Rogen." The plastic prevents me from shaking hands. "I'm the new hire for Mike."

"Ah! Mike's new kid!" Her eyes light up.

"Good to meet you, Nick! Come on in!" The woman lets me through the door as the locking mechanism clicks and grinds like I'm entering a bunker. It thuds closed and locks behind me.

"I'm Kathy." We shake hands.

"Nice to meet you."

She nods. "Let me show you around the office, and then I'll let Joyce give you a tour of the warehouse where you'll be working.

"Alright."

I follow her down a large, open hallway and notice that the inside of the building looks a lot nicer than the outside.

We enter a large room with three cubicles "Here is where the lowly peons like myself work."

She laughs and I do the same.

No, this isn't going to be bad at all. Maybe a job will get me out of this slump I am in. Now that I am done with school, my days are all too free and I need to keep myself busy.

"If you ever need me"—she points to the corner cubicle—"I'll be there. The rest of these desks are for the cash office, PR, that sorta stuff. Nothing you have to worry too much about."

We walk over to a side office door and Kathy knocks gently. I can't imagine her knocking any harder than a tap.

"Come on in," a husky voice responds.

I suck in a laugh as I enter.

Everything is Pepsi-stamped. The clock. The posters. The toys on the desk. The wall calendar. Hell, it's actually pretty freaky.

"This is Nick," Kathy's voice sounds like a small mouse. "The new hire."

The woman sitting down is huge. A great frog of a woman with tattered hair that went gray long before it should have. She looks mad as hell.

I gulp.

Can I have Kathy show me around? The question dies in my throat.

Joyce grunts. "Welcome aboard, kiddo. Mike's out for the next few days on a business trip. So, you got me instead. Let's go have ourselves a tour, shall we?" After struggling from her chair, she waddles ahead of me and I follow.

Kathy waves. "See you soon!"

I mouth a thank you and catch up to Joyce with a few strides.

We leave the office in silence.

When we make it the warehouse section of the building, I am shocked. The atmosphere changes completely. Like that part in *The Wizard of Oz* where everything shifts from black and white to color. Except this is the opposite. We go from colorful offices to a grey, static warehouse.

We walk past the guarded money clerk and Joyce explains to me that this is where all the drivers leave their days' earnings. She also tells me not to worry about it. It isn't my job.

The room before the double doors is the lunch room. I use the term very loosely. There's a candy machine, a Pepsi machine, and one of those terrible road-stop espresso machine that has an added soup option.

I attempt to break the ice as we walk by.

I point to the soda machine. "I take it I can't get an ice-cold Coke from there during my breaks, eh?"

I smile to signify I'm joking.

Her penguin stride halts.

She turns with a heavy expression. More so than her usual.

"We don't say the 'c' word here."

She spins around and keeps waddling.

I hold back a laugh.

This is not starting out well.

⌇

The warehouse is bitterly cold even though it's midway through September. We walk the edges of the warehouse on strips of yellow paint that signify to forklift drivers not to run over the people crossing them.

How comforting.

We stride past the stacks and stacks of assorted soda products. The roar of distant forklifts barely drowns out the beat of country music from the speakers nearby. A forklift zooms past us. A bearded man smiles brightly and waves. I wave back.

"That's Dennis. He's been here since the seventies."

"Wow." I follow Dennis on his forklift until he pulls a sharp turn and disappears behind a wall of soda.

"He's a good guy, you'll like him."

We continue along the yellow brick road until we stop in front of five loading docks in the front of the warehouse.

"Here's where the large trucks come in to get their orders. Usually for major chains and superstores. The Wal-Marts and such. The little trucks for delivering to convenience stores get checked in out back."

"Part of your job will be to keep track, both written and electronically, of the truck's inventory throughout the day. Make sure nothing gets lost, stolen. That sort of thing."

I nod.

We continue down an aisle full of pallets containing oddly stacked blue Lego things. Joyce picks one up with her index finger and thumb. She looks like she's picking up the most disgusting thing she's ever seen. Her face is twisted.

"These are shells."

"Shells?" I feel my stomach rumble. Nothing seems very glamorous here.

"Shells are what we use to keep the soda in to transport them to the stores. There's a different shell type for every product we sell."

She drops the shell and it clatters on the ground.

"Part of your job will be to sort and stack them accordingly. Then you'll wrap them up with cellophane and forklift drivers like Dennis will take them away."

I nod again, speechless.

Our next stop is what Joyce refers to as the Recovery Area. Two people my age are already there. One, a teenager who looks like a black-haired Chris Farley, is twisting caps off of bottles. When he twists all of the bottles in a shell, he pours them into a large drain on the floor. The other man is throwing cans into the small machine located beside the drain. Next to him, a constant churning noise emanates off a large, dirty vat. Flies circle overhead.

"You'll spend most of your time here. It's basically where you'll dig through broken cases of product, pull out and clean the good ones, and repackage them to sell."

"Why is that worker twisting bottle caps?"

Joyce's eyebrows arch.

"Oh, what Christian's doing? He's throwing out the bad pop."

"Bad pop?"

"Expired stuff. You can't legally dump it straight away because of the chemicals in it. So we have to unscrew the caps and unload them into that vat. When the vat completely fills, we dump in chemicals to neutralize the PH level, and then dump it."

"We twist every bottle cap off?" I suddenly want to run as far away from this place as I can.

"Yep." She looks ready to say something else, but stops.

I follow her out the back door. A whole side of the courtyard is dedicated to rows of shells that come off the trucks.

"You'll be doing inventory checks and shells out here as well. It gets kinda nasty here with the rain and everything, but you'll be fine."

She turns to me. "Got it?"

"Got it."

She smiles for the first time since we met.

I bet she can't wait to get back to her comfy office chair.

"Good. Now, we'll go back to the offices and you have a couple of hours of training videos to watch."

I follow in silence and wonder what the hell I am doing here.

Chapter 20

Cue the Casino Chase (December 2004)

"So where do you think she is?" Dad asks me.

I lean forward in the living room chair.

"We both know where she is."

His eyebrows arch as he, too, leans forward in the chair across from me. I look at him and nod.

First, all the years of depression, of mental hospitals, of shock treatments, and now, this.

"I'll go find her," I tell him with a sigh.

Mom has been gone for two days now; her weekend benders are getting more and more frequent.

"You know how to find her?" he asks me.

I know exactly where she is.

"Yeah. I have a pretty good idea," I reply.

I don't bother to grab a coat on the way out.

⤳

I feel more angry then concerned as I drive back toward Tacoma where I'd gotten off of work at Pepsi over an hour ago. I head straight for the Indian reservation. When I pull into the parking lot, I'm surprised at how many cars are there. Must be thousands.

I take my time and drive down each parking aisle. I find Mom's yellow Volkswagen easily. Gamblers may have loved the lights and action of casinos, but their car colors sure didn't show it. Almost all the cars in the lot are a dull gray. Mom's car is easy to spot.

It's freezing when I get out of my car.

Damn. I should have gotten that coat.

The casino itself is massive, taking up at least four or five blocks in every direction but up. Though I'm sure they have plans to build in that direction with the next house deed they receive in a back room. Its bright neon sign flashes a pre-programmed light show fifty feet above my head into the sky. Might as well try to advertise to planes too, right?

As I near the doors, I can see through to the color wheel of a lobby; a color wheel on drugs. I go straight up to the muscular security guard who doesn't open the door for me.

"ID please." Her voice is husky, a strong match to her massive body. Lying has never been one of my strong suits, and a casino is definitely not a place to lay down suits you don't trust. I'm not about to start now.

"I'm only eighteen, but I'm actually here to find my mother. If it's acceptable, you can escort me through or have another staff member help me to—"

"Sorry kiddo. No minors. No exceptions."

"Fine." The cold is bitter and I'm in no mood to argue. "Can you at least page her to come to the front, please?"

"Honey, there's a lot of fronts here."

This is ridiculous.

"To whatever front *this* is then."

With an annoyed look, she nods. I move aside as a couple excuses themselves between us to the warmth that is bleeding from the inside. "What's her name?"

"Sandy Rogen."

"Sandy Rogen? Okay, I'll go give it a try."

Try? What the hell is so hard about a simple page?

She closes the door and talks to another co-worker who leaves a second later and heads toward the lobby. The husky woman turns to me and nods again. She says something to me through the glass, but the roar and jingle of slot machines dominates my ear drums.

I sit down on the concrete bench and wait. The security guard comes back outside and turns to stone again; a gargoyle guarding her usual spot.

My body is beginning to numb. I try my best to not look like an epileptic and keep my tongue in between my chattering teeth. Even as cold as I am, I still can feel my blood boiling.

This is my weekend. And I'm here, freezing my ass off outside some Indian casino waiting for what? Another excuse? Another sorry?

I let out a sigh and watch as the steam drifts up into the air.

Why am I even here?

"Hey kid." I lift my head to a woman standing in front of me. A whirlwind of smoke twists across her face as she takes a drag from her cigarette. "Didn't let you in, uh?" Her face is tan, with as many wrinkles as a nice dress shirt that has yet to meet an iron.

"Nope." I roll my eyes. "Sucks."

She lets out a dry, raspy laugh as her black hair bounces over her thin face. She can't be older than mid-thirties, though the bags under her eyes make her look as if she has been at the casino for days.

"Yeah, I remember being around your age. I had to find other ways of getting in."

I laugh to be polite.

"So what's your name, cutie?"

Oh man, is she hitting on me?

"Nick. Nice to meet you." I nod my head instead of extending my hand to shake.

"So how old are you, Nick?"

I suddenly feel very awkward. I shift my eyes away from hers and notice a person, distant in the parking lot, sprinting through the lines of cars like an Olympic runner. I squint.

It's Mom.

I bound up. "Nice meeting you!" I blurt out and begin running toward Mom. I don't hear a response behind me.

I dart through the cars like a skillful knife, cutting through departing cars whose curses and horns blare through the night.

Mom makes it about a hundred feet away from her car before I close the gap and dash out in front of her. I wasn't named one of the best short-distance runners in track for nothing.

"Nick!" She stops. A contorted smile spreads across her face. "What are you doing here?" Her eyes are wild with mania. She holds her purse in her hands, things spilling out of the top.

"Give me the card!" I shout. My blood has already reached its boiling point. "Now!" I put my hand out.

She tries to step back and forth to get past me, but I move in a mechanical sway with her movements.

She explodes with manic laughter. "Come on now. I was just having a good time."

"Give me the *fucking* card! Now!" I scream. I have never felt so enraged in my entire life.

Mom's smile disappears.

"Fine." She reaches into her purse and takes out her Visa and plops it into my hands.

My fingers wrap around the card like a spider. I try to say something more, but can't think of anything else to say. I storm off to my car. It isn't twenty seconds later before I'm back on the highway and heading toward home. My speedometer hits eighty-five.

It is all a joke to her.

I slam by hand against the steering wheel.

At that moment, driving so wild down the road, I lose all respect for the mother I had taken care of for my entire life.

Chapter 21

One and the Same

I stand completely still in the night after closing the car door. Maybe it is the cold that brings my anger down a notch. Or the silent drive home. Whatever it is, I feel guilt slowly replacing my anger.

What just happened?

I have never lashed out like that in my entire life. Never have I let my anger flow so freely to my words and actions. I went to the casino to find Mom and bring her home. That's it. I didn't go to blow up at her in the middle of a crowded parking lot.

I drag myself to the front door, the frost-laden grass crunching underneath my footsteps. What triggered me? Was it sitting in the cold for an hour, or did I snap when I saw her make a break for her car so that she wouldn't have to encounter me?

I open the front door.

Or was it something deeper? An anger I had withheld for years now?

All the lights in my house are off, save the one in the living room, which gives an eerie glow and outline to the hallway where I take off my shoes. Dad is already asleep. Working at Boeing and waking up at three in the morning is no easy task. Had he been blessed with a better temper, I'm sure he would have been the one that went to find Mom instead of me. But I am the negotiator of the family; the level-headed one.

And I failed.

I sit down in one of the living room armchairs and sink into the cushions. I'm strangely calm. It is an odd feeling after such an outburst.

I can't tell how long I sit there. The Adderall in my bloodstream is dissipating from the morning dose and I'm crashing quickly. I hear the front door squeak open and close. No slam.

The Mom that walks into the living room isn't the manic one from earlier. No wild eyes, no twisted smile. Nor is it the depressed mother with droopy eyes and a sagging mouth. The Mom that walks in is the one who looks like she has been through a car accident that barely left her alive. Her eyes are full cups of tears, tipping and spilling down her reddened cheeks. Her mouth holds a shaking frown. When she first steps into the room, I look up in shock.

What have I done?

She says nothing, nor attempts to do so. She moves like a sloth to the chair opposite me, and with the utmost care, sits down. Unlike me, she doesn't fall back into the cushions.

I begin to say I'm sorry, but she interrupts me with a struggled sentence. "I wish to God that you would have been given a different mother. One who wasn't so sick. So disappointing."

For a moment, the house is filled with her crying. I don't know what to say.

"No," I say, shaking my head as tears form in my eyes. I lean out of my chair and go over to her. "No, no, no, no," I keep repeating, at a lost for better words. I wrap my arms around her. She feels cold and small. Any anger I had earlier has fizzled away. I am now back to the role I know well.

"No, that's not true. This is my fault. I shouldn't have blown up at you like that."

She lifts her head. Her cheeks are glazed over with smashed tears. "I'm a failure."

"No," I whisper. I grab her head and tuck it into my shoulder. "You aren't a failure. You raised me didn't you?" I try to smile.

"You raised yourself while I was a basket case in a mental—"

"You have a problem and I'm here for you. You beat depression. You can beat this."

She shakes her head. "I don't know how to stop."

Maybe that was why I got so mad at her. I'm just like her.

I'm sure I have said the same thing once. Here I am, addicted to drugs and she is addicted to gambling.

I hug harder and know why I have become so angry. Looking at Mom now is like looking at a mirror. We both struggle; I just never let anyone know about my problems. I never want to get anyone else involved in my own vices.

"Whether you know it or not," I say, "I know what you're going through. Addiction is a horrible thing."

"You don't even know how much I spent."

I smile. "It's just money. That's all it is."

She tries to smile back.

"I would never choose another mother. Without you, I wouldn't be who I am today. We're a team. And I will love you no matter what happens."

Her head falls back to my shoulder.

"I'm so sorry for yelling at you."

"I deserved it."

I drop back from the hug and look her in the eyes.

"You deserve nothing but thanks."

She rolls her eyes.

I stand up and take back my seat. "And we'll get through this."

I really do mean *we*. I have my own demons to face and she has hers.

We talk late into the night. After she goes to bed, I go to my room, turn on my lava lamp, find my walkman, and down as many extra Clorazapam pills as I can find.

A walking contradiction at its finest.

Mom is ready to face her demons. She has the inner strength and I am proud of her for that. Mom has Dad and me to help her out. I, on the other hand, have no one to help me. I am too afraid to ask anyone for help, even my own parents; so instead, I choose to continue sinking.

Chapter 22

A One-Way Conversation (January 2005)

Driving to Pepsi is always the same. I know down to the exact minute when I'll arrive at my parking spot. I get behind the same white SUV every afternoon. He goes sixty-five and it makes it easy to just follow him as people slide out of his way.

I'm on River Road, a long stretch of highway that goes on for miles. The river runs parallel next to me. On the left are broken-down houses, trailers, and dozens of drive-thru smoke shops.

They say this is the most dangerous road in all of Washington. The various DUI memorials plastered on passing street signs attest to this.

It starts to rain.

What an ugly road.

I twist the cap off my coffee container.

Red wine pours down into my mouth.

I flick on the wipers.

My face cringes at the taste of the cold wine and a sudden surge of guilt passes through me.

"What?" I say to my passenger's seat.

I imagine God is sitting there. A face scrunched in disappointment.

"It's not like I'm driving drunk. I'm not drunk."

The pothole I usually miss sends the tiny car bouncing.

My passenger is silent. Invisible.

He doesn't respond. Doesn't need to.

"What's happening to me, God?" A tear scrolls down my cheek. "What happened to that kid who dreamed of being a writer? Why can't I shake this? I go home every goddamn—," I stop myself. "My day consists of waking up, popping some Adderall to wake me up from all the Clorazapam of the previous night. Why do I have to do this just to go to work?"

"I mean, I'm more than this! I was the top of my class and here I am twisting off bottle caps for a living!"

I take another gulp from my wine and watch a large billboard blur by me on the right. It tells me to find my meaning in life by becoming a mentor to underprivileged kids.

I laugh. If there were ever a perfect use for the word ironic, this would be that moment. I turn to my invisible passenger.

"Tell me God, where the hell did I go wrong?"

I shake the container toward God. "And why can't I just stop? It'd be so easy to just pour this out the window! But why can't I do it if it's that simple?"

He doesn't answer. He stares at me instead.

I look away, ashamed.

I keep my monologue going as I pass the Indian reservation I chased Mom through so many months ago.

"I still remember, back when I was clean of all this shit, that mountain climber in Switzerland. Craig. Asked me why I wanted to become a writer. And here I am, two years later and I still don't have an answer to that haunting question."

I wipe my tears and turn onto the highway entrance ramp.

"What a failure I am."

My passenger doesn't say a thing.

"Pop goes outdated." I'm talking in a trance. "Thousands a day in fact. And I twist off every cap. Every single one. And dump it into a vat to mix it with chemicals so it can legally be drained. Between every couple of bottles or so, I stack and organize the shells that the pop will get shipped to the stores in. The shells are usually placed outside *ampm* stores until the driver can return to pick them up. Most have urine on them. Needles in some. A positive home pregnancy test in another—"

God knows all this already.

I want to say it all again to him though. Make sure He really sees how much of a failure of a son He has in me.

The wine is helping in this convincing argument.

"I also check the trucks' inventories using third grade math. Sometimes, Mike, the big boss, mixes it up. I'll scrub the floors. Paint the bigwig offices. When I really want a change of pace though, I repackage cans. Ha, I'm so doped up at work, I don't care anymore. When I get home, I drink myself to sleep."

I look to my passenger's seat. God looks to be asleep.

"I haven't touched a pen in months. So much for a career in writing, eh, God?"

More wine gurgles down my throat.

"You know God, Dennis, that old forklift driver pulled me aside the other day and said to me, 'Nick, what the fuck are you still doing here?'"

"Making money," I told him.

"He dug his finger into my chest and for once, I didn't see that famous Dennis smile. 'Please,' he said, 'get out. Go to school. You're better than this. Get out of this hole while you can.'"

"Some speech, uh?"

I pull into the Pepsi parking lot and grab a gravel parking spot in the back next to the Humane Society.

I chug what is left of the wine. I twitch and shake my head.

"Everyone tells me they see this shining star in me. That I'm different." I pull the keys from the ignition.

"So what that I helped my Mom? What else would I have done? Am I really that different? Am I really that special? What the hell am

I supposed to do? What's my purpose in any of this? God, I feel like a fucking modern-day Tolstoy."

I'm buzzed and the world feels better.

"The answer is no, God. I'm not special and I don't have any real purpose worth caring about. In case you didn't know."

I jump out of the car. "See you later, God. I got some bottle caps to twist."

I slam the car door on God and head to work.

Chapter 23

A Cry for Help (March 2005)

I have known Travis for a few years now. Actually, I had met him my junior year at Sumner High School. He was campaigning for class treasurer at the time. When I first met him, he was this huge loudmouth who cracked vulgar jokes every chance he could get. He was the opposite of my demeanor, but for some reason we clicked. He cracked his sex jokes, and I rattled off my sarcastic ones. With that, we became friends before we knew it.

And now here we were, sitting in a Starbucks, still stuck in the same town we'd grown up in, with high school long over with. I was working at Pepsi, and he was slaving away for "The Man" at a cable company. Entwined with our jokes, we also now shared the common thread of hatred for our jobs. And as much as I despised mine, I had recently become a minimum-wage workaholic, so I never got a chance to see him. But we tried our best to hit up as many concerts as we could, and sneak into a few movies here and there. When I hung out with him, I felt like the kid I never was.

Travis was a good friend. Someone I trusted. Funny thing is, he was the only one I told my problems to. Not that I ever listened to his answers. I was still that independent child at heart.

I take a sip from my mocha and let my eyes wander as I talk. As brave as I feel talking with Travis, I'm still afraid to lock eyes.

I'm not the least bit proud of myself.

"I don't know," I continue the conversation. "I don't how to explain it, man. The Clorazapam and all the other antipsychotics. They're literally erasing my days. It's like that flashy thing in *Men in Black* that erases your memory. What a drug to become addicted to make it through the day, huh?" I sigh. "I pop a few Adderall in the morning to recover from the drug hangover from the night before, race through my day, take a few downers on my way to work, get drunk at home—"

I take another sip. "Then rinse and repeat."

Travis looks at me with disappointment. "Why don't you just quit that job of yours? That seems to be the problem right there. It's sucking the life out of you."

I laugh. "It's not just the job."

"Oh yeah? What is it then?"

"It's everything. In high school, you knew me. I was the good kid. But you know all the times I said 'fuck it' to college? All those days I said I would put my life on hold and sulk around a bit before figuring my life out? All those times I didn't plan for my future? Well, they caught up with me. I'm stuck working at Pepsi. I've pushed my dreams aside. I wanted to become a writer. But now, I hate everything I write, and—" I let my sentence die off. I sigh once more. "You want to know the problem, Travis? What's holding me back? I just don't know how to get my dreams back. I have forgotten who it was I wanted to be."

His eyebrows rise in surprise. "Wow. That sure was deep." He chuckles. "It's simple, buddy. Quit. Go to school. Write. You got so much skill in English, I don't understand why you don't have a best seller by now!"

"God, I wish it was that simple." I suck down what is left of my mocha and let the excess chocolate drip down my throat. I put the cup back on the checkered table and look toward Travis. "You see, Pepsi is like this safety net. I quit once, but then I didn't know what to do with my time. And now"—I grab the coffee cup back up and hold it. I have no idea why, but I feel the need to have something in my hand—"I'm an addict. I'm surprised I don't have some kind of crazy tic by now."

I twitch for effect. "I'm like all the people in school I told myself I'd never be like. I'm such a damn people pleaser. I have to make every single person happy. If I quit, that screws over a lot of the people I work with."

Travis throws back his head and lets out an exaggerated sigh that rivals the espresso machines that are whirling and grinding in the background. "Will you shut up now? Honestly, Nick. You're right. All you do in your life is try and help others. That's how you were raised. Always others before yourself. Hell," he raises his coffee cup in the air, "I even know you'll demand to pay the bill for this coffee."

He puts his cup down on the table and leans in. I've never seen him more serious in my life. "But all this helping is destroying you."

I close my eyes. This is not what I want to hear. I know he is right.

"But Nick, one of these days you're going to have to help yourself for once. Or at least let someone help you. Otherwise—" he trails off.

I try to laugh off his answer, but can't.

"I know," I choke out. I open my eyes. "I know."

His eyebrows arch. "But what do I know?" He sinks back in his chair and rubs his eyes. "Speaking of helping people, how's the family? How's your mom doing?"

"She's good." Even with Travis I let out the automatic response I have used since before I can remember. I am glad, though, that he has decided not to pursue his lecture.

"I mean the real answer."

Then again, I'm a horrible liar.

"She's doing a lot better. Stabilized."

"You know, you're a lot like your mom. She got through her shit, and you'll get through yours."

I ease my body into the cushions.

"I love you, man. But Travis"—I look him in the eyes—"you're wrong."

〜

It's an hour later, and we're still talking.

"So wait, let me get this straight," Travis says as he shakes his head back and forth. "It all starts with a suicide?"

"Yeah."

Travis laughs with me as he takes a sip from his coffee. "That doesn't make any sense at all. You know that, right?"

"Sure it does."

"So the main character—" he trails off.

"Chris," I say.

"So, Chris is driving at the beginning of the story, sobbing like crazy for some strange reason that the reader doesn't know about yet. And then, we he gets home, before he gets out of the car, he tries to compose himself, but can't, so pulls this gun out of nowhere—"

"The glove compartment," I correct him with a smile.

"Out of the glove compartment, and then proceeds to blow his brains out."

I nod for him to continue.

"But then, right afterwards, he gets out of his car and heads inside his house. Alive."

"Yep, you got it all right." I sit back in the sofa chair, inhale the coffee smell, and smile.

It was a brilliant idea for the start of my book. It had been almost a year now since I had been in Mr. Brown's high school office talking about my future. I didn't have any good material for writing then, and now wasn't much different. Except now I had a plot line growing in my head. I just needed to write it down.

That is a start, right?

Travis shakes his head. "To be honest, that makes no fucking sense to me. At all, man."

I sit up in my chair. This is going to take some explaining.

"You're thinking of suicide all wrong here."

"Wrong?" His large face crinkles up. "When you blow your brains to pieces, you pretty much die. Or end up retarded because half your brain is gone."

"Right. But you're only looking at the physical suicide."

Now he really looks confused. For a moment, I feel the urge to stop the conversation. Maybe it is a bad idea. Maybe I'm not the great writer everyone told me I was.

"Physical suicide? Opposed to what?"

"A mental suicide."

"Uh huh. A mental one." He rolls his eyes.

"It's all a metaphor, man. Mental suicide stands for suicide of the brain. It's the death of your ideas, hopes, dreams—all that stuff. And it can happen by choice or without your consent." I take a drink from my second mocha of the day. It's making my Adderall work double time. But even with the drug, it's hard to explain my idea. "Your heart still beats, but you're empty inside. You've killed off what makes you, you."

He is silent. His large hands rotate around his cup before he pushes back the hair from in front of his eyes. "Like giving up on your life."

"Exactly!" I'm excited. If Travis understood where I'm coming from—

"Like you working at Pepsi."

I turn away. Travis has a habit of bluntness … and of being right.

He smirks. "But hey, not bad, man. Not bad at all. But it still doesn't explain the gun at all."

"It's all in his head, as though he's killing off his dreams without doing anything about it."

"But why would someone willfully commit"—he makes quotation marks in the air with his fingers—"mental suicide?"

I look away again.

"I mean it's a great start to a story, and with your talent in writing I'm sure it'll be nothing but awesome. But what do you plan to do next in the story?"

I meet his glance and am glad I don't have to answer his first question.

"I have it all outlined. It's actually going to be a sort of sci-fi-ish novel with a man who can live forever but wishes he could die. And he meets up with this kid who lost his mother and gave up on his life as—" I let my words die off. Now that I have said the entire plot aloud, it sounds dumb and unoriginal. "Never mind, it's a stupid idea. I'm sorry about wasting your time. I was just excited to actually have the inspiration to write."

Travis's eyes look like they are going to pop out of his head. His arms flail like a cartoon character.

"Goddamn, Nick! Just write the thing! It sounds great!" He thrusts his hand at me in the air with every word he says. "Don't do that pussy thing and give up on it before you even begin it. I swear, man, you're your own worse critic!"

He puts his coffee down and straightens up in his chair. "Look at me. My name's Nick and I have such great talent and ideas, but I'm just a big pussy and whine about how lame I am."

Mocha almost sprays from my mouth. Travis slips back into his chair.

After I control my laughter, I notice he isn't smiling. "Maybe you're right. It is a waste of my time being here. You call me up and we come here and you first ramble on about how drugs are destroying your life and then you go on and on about a book idea to me you're never even going to write. All for what? Are you actually going to even listen to me?" He looks around the coffee shop, empty except for the cute barista he attempted to hit on when we first came in. He turns his attention back to me.

"But I want to tell you something before I go, even if you decide not to do it. All I want you to do right now is listen."

Travis sighs and put down his coffee cup.

"We all have our problems, Nick. And sooner or later, we all have to deal with them. Skeletons in the closest don't really ever go away. You have to learn how to deal with them. That's the secret."

God, when had Travis become such a shrink?

I feel like I need to pay him for advice I'll never use. But I asked it for it. I invited him here. And now I feel like a scolded child. My eyes are cast to the ground and I fight the urge to get up and walk out and leave the rest of his long-winded speech to fall on deaf ears.

It's all a bunch of shit anyway. Something made up to make me feel better. Isn't that what friends are for? To tell you everything is going to be alright and make up lies and speeches to convince you?

I sigh. But, dammit, something inside me, somewhere, knows he is right.

"And Jesus, Nick, you of all people. You've lived more lifetimes than any nineteen-year-old I've ever known. You helped your mother through depression. You backpacked around Europe. Hell, man, you even won a damn fridge on *The Price Is Right*!" He leans toward me. "And pretty soon you're going to China and you'll be an older brother, man."

The adoption subject. Not something I was fond of. My parents had decided to adopt years ago. But only now was it finally looking as though it were actually going to happen. We were even sent the little girl's picture last week so we knew what she looked like. I didn't know what to think of the whole thing. It was a giant change, but I had bigger things to worry about.

Travis keeps going with his monologue. "If it were anyone else, I wouldn't bother. But you can get out of this slump."

I look up. I want to tell him how wrong he is. How far I have really fallen. I want to tell him to go fuck off for being so helpful. Instead,

I whisper what I have been thinking during our entire conversation. What I have secretly, even to me, brought him here for; to get me to ask the simple question I've never wanted to utter to anyone. Never wanted to admit how weak I was.

"Where do I start?"

He seems more than ready for my question. "Put faith in yourself. Go back to school. Start writing. You have a great idea for a novel that you just told me. Work with it." Travis begins putting on his coat as he talks. "Just don't forget who you were meant to be."

"And who's that?"

"Someone who will change the world." I've never heard Travis sound more serious.

He has to be joking. "Don't get all sappy on me. You know how stupid that sounds? Seriously, they only say shit like that in the movies."

He ignores me. "You want to know something, Nick?"

I don't answer. I know he'll tell me no matter what I say.

"I think, no, actually." He shakes his head. "I know, for a fact, that no matter how far you fall down that hole you dug of yours, I don't think you'll ever make it too deep."

"What the hell does that mean?"

"Honestly, I don't think anything can stop you. Even yourself. I think no matter how hard you try to destroy yourself, you'll make it in the end, no matter what. You have that much talent."

I don't know what to say. What do you say to something like that? That no matter how much I fuck up my life, I have the inner strength to pull through?

Travis gets up from his seat. I almost grab him and shove him back down. He can't leave. Not now.

"Because that's the person you are and always will be. Whether you accept it or not." He throws a five dollar bill down on the table. "Thanks for the coffee."

He smiles at the girl in the corner, nods me a good-bye, and leaves. I watch his car drive away until the jingle from above the exit has long faded away into the stream of blundering coffee machines, churning on high in preparation for the afternoon caffeine fiends.

I sigh to the empty seat across from me.

Chapter 24

My Fifteen Minutes (April 2005)

I am fifteen minutes early for work. Like always.

For the last six months, I have driven the same route back and forth, day in and day out, to work. The SUV on River Road seems a lot like me. Both of us are trapped in an endless cycle of the mundane.

I'm never late for work, and for the fifteen minutes before I get out of my car, I use the time to sit as I am now, staring at the peeling white bricks of the Pepsi warehouse and dwelling on how much I hate it here.

What a sad loser I've become.

I turn off the ignition.

My mind is an empty slate. I should be thinking about writing more, or going back to school, or what I'm going to do this coming Friday night like any other regular nineteen-year-old kid. But I don't. My thoughts are nonexistent, and to be honest, that feels more disturbing than anything I can imagine.

This job, this life I have now—this is was what it is doing. Erasing my dreams and replacing them with emptiness.

I am being reduced to compromising, and I'm not doing a fucking thing to stop it.

I rummage through my pockets and find two green Clorazapam pills.

I try to choke out a laugh.

Drugging away the nothingness I have become.

How cliché.

I dry swallow them both.

It'd be at least an hour before the effect hit me; that pleasant, dream-like feeling.

It makes my mind turn to slush.

But really, what is wrong with being a zombie for a zombie job?

By tomorrow, I'd hardly remember a thing I did while I was on it. Funny how easy it is to get a hold of drugs when you really want them.

Stuck by complacency.

Story of my life.

I am digging my own hole to fall into. No cries for help. I am the one to help other people with their problems. Not my own.

"I'm a goddamn hypocrite."

I sigh and check my watch. Five minutes 'til.

I cut the music and get out of my car. I walk to the steel fence and flash my reader badge. It thanks me in with a green light. It's light outside for an April afternoon. Usually, it's still pouring rain. I grab the steel door, swing it open, and enter the darkness.

The door behind me thuds closed. The mechanics usually lead to a gentle, automated shut, but they are broken and rusted. The brightness of the outside diminishes, not unlike a solar eclipse blocking out the sun. When the lock clicks, all outside light is gone.

I blink several times and let my eyes readjust to the dark.

Back to the tomb.

To the left of me is the beginning of the two-liter row. Pop stacked up to the nearly twenty-foot ceiling. It looks a lot like Costco.

I walk to the offices in the opposite corner of the warehouse, passing by my main section of work, the Recovery Area. The place where heaps of broken product from sleep-deprived forklift driver accidents awaits to be sorted, washed, and repackaged. Oh, and it is where we do the bottle twisting. Thousands of bottles a day of bad pop, and I and two other co-workers have the fabulous job of twisting every single cap off and pouring it down into a machine that dilutes the chemicals to make it safe to dispose of.

If I didn't know better, I sometimes think I am in heaven—

I give a wave and smile to Christian. He waves back from where he is standing next to the can bailer. The can bailer is the machine we put all the expired pop cans in. It smashes the cans down into one of those tiny blocks you see impound yards do to cars in the movies. Every smash sends pop flying everywhere. By the time I get home every evening, my pants are coated in it. Sometimes I have to beat at them before work just to be able to walk normally.

Christian is the janitor for Pepsi, only a tad older than me, but he frequently comes back and helps Recovery.

All in all, the Recovery Area is a happy home to flies and carpal tunnel syndrome.

I keep my stride and don't stop to chat. I glance over to Ian who is stacking the Pepsi shells a few rows down from the Recovery Area. He is in the middle of at least twenty pallets, and counting off to make sure he's stacked enough on each one. Stacking shells is a lot like adult Legos. You have your two-liter shells, your one-liters, your twenty-ouncers, your one-point-fives, and so on. Ian has his oversized gloves on, because half the fun of the shells is the piss and God knows what else on them from sitting too long at the side of a convenience store.

How the hell did I get so lucky to be stuck here?

I give him a curt smile. He returns with his own goofy copy.

Ian had taken my job after my first attempt at quitting Pepsi failed a few months back. But I wasn't going to college and I hadn't written anything worthwhile in months that would have remotely made me think I could be a writer. I had nothing. So I crawled back here and Mike decided to keep us both on. Ian was a different sort of kid. A little slow. Not mentally retarded by any means, but I wouldn't put it past him to be straddling that border of sanity. Along with him and my other womanizing co-worker Shane, we made a mismatched Three Musketeers.

But Ian knew his sports. A talent I could see was being wasted here. He could rattle on about every significant sports figure for hours at a time. He frequently did. And every opportunity I got, I tried to convince him to go to school.

He never listened.

I get to the main work area where the lunch room, bathroom, and time clock are. I grab my card and swipe it through. I don't even bother to look at the time.

Dennis walks out of the break room and smiles at me. His tiny head is engulfed by his smile.

"Quitting yet?" Dennis asks, patting me on the shoulder as he walks past.

Dennis asks me this every day. He often tells me he sees talent spilling out of my sides.

"Not yet, Dennis." I laugh. Dennis is a good man and I don't have the heart to tell him that I don't have any plans of leaving soon.

I continue up the stairs. I'm in worker prison; each clank of steel a reminder of the slow, dragging day ahead.

I open the door and hit the wall of air conditioning and brightly lit offices. I look over the first cubicle to say hi to Kathy, but her seat is empty.

Next to Kathy's desk is the forklift driver supervisor, Ken.

"Hey Nick." He smiles. His frame is like my own, but his back is arched from years of forklift driving and lifting. Rumor has it he'll be retiring in a year or so, even though he is relatively young.

Standing in front of him is Mike, my main boss. I can see the reflection of the lights bounce off his bald head. His pudgy face turns to me. His large eyes are cold.

"What's going on?" I ask.

Mike sighs and turns to Ken, then back to me.

"Can I see you in my office, Nick?"

"Sure." I grab my radio from the corner of the office and follow him down the hallway.

I sit down in one of the chairs set across from him, trying my best to not get distracted by the abundance of Pepsi paraphernalia littering his cubicle-like office.

"It's Ian again," he says, skipping any conversational fluff.

I put my head down and say nothing.

"I shouldn't be telling you this, but—" He trails off until I look up and then makes an inch sign with his stubby fingers. "He's this close to being fired."

"What'd he do this time?"

Mike laughs. "Where do I start? He's not counting right and sure as heck can't handle himself on Mondays when you're off. I mean, I can't have someone that needs you supervising them to do their job, right?"

I rub my eyes.

I like Ian. He is a good kid. I make it a habit to nag him to put the money he is making away for college (something I'm not doing), so he can use his knowledge in sports and get the hell out of here. I am sure that if I have a little more time, I can convince him. Just a few more months of persuasion.

"Let me talk with him."

Mike has piercing eyes. Eyes that do his talking for him.

"Give him another chance," I say.

I can tell his mind is churning, his eyes darting back and forth across my face.

"Okay, Nick. One. But just one. And know that if he—"

"I know Mike. I know. Thanks." He nods and I excuse myself.

I run into Kathy barreling up the stairs on my way down back to the warehouse. Ken is standing in the middle of us.

"Goddamn Ian can't understand a thing I tell him!"

Ken lets Kathy lead the conversation. He knows it's better to stay on her good side.

"He's just an idiot. But you and Nick here think he'll get better."

I keep walking past them.

"He won't, Ken. I'm telling you. He won't."

I should say something. Kathy is my favorite middle-level boss, and I should tell her to keep her voice down. Voices drift with ease in warehouses.

But it's a should-have and I'm already walking away.

I reach the shell aisle and lean onto a finished, shrink-wrapped pallet that is ready to be forklifted away.

"Ian."

He pops out from behind a nearby block of shells.

"It's the Nickster!"

"Ian." I sigh. "Come here."

He gallops over to me. His energy is amazing. Then again, so was mine when I first started working here. He hasn't hit the "not caring about your life" phase yet.

I can't leave him in the dark.

"You need to get out of here."

"What?"

"Go to school or something. Anywhere but here."

He laughs, but his eyes don't play along. "Not this speech again. Come on now! For what? Both of us know I'm not smart enough to go."

"Shut up, man. Go into radio broadcasting. Become a sportscaster. At least do something."

He looks down and shakes his head.

"Ian, look at me." I'm the disappointed parent.

He raises his head.

"Get the hell out of this hole. You don't want to be stuck here like me."

"You're not stuck here."

I almost laugh.

"I am, but that's not the point. You aren't yet. I'll help you look for schools. I'll help with—"

"Fine." He's getting agitated. "But I have to stay here and earn enough money first."

"No!" I bark. I feel horrible that I can't tell him he is on the verge of being fired. "No," I say again, calmer this time. "That's what I did. And I'm still here. Take out a loan. Do whatever you have to do, but get out."

He laughs again. "Thanks Nick, but I'm staying for now."

He continues with the stacking.

"Fine, Ian, fine. But listen, you have any questions on something here, or something goes wrong, come to me first, not Mike or Kathy or Ken. Okay?"

"Why would I do that?"

I swallow hard. "Just do it."

"Wouldn't that get you in trouble instead?"

"Ian. Just don't worry about it, okay?"

"Okay, geez. Whatever you say boss!" He salutes me and grins.

Hell, at least I tried.

Walking away, I can feel a drowsiness come over me. The drugs, and my workday, are starting hand in hand.

Chapter 25

Through Closed Eyes (May 2005)

They say boredom makes kids do drugs. Sad to say, but there might be a little truth in that simple nugget of information.

It's Saturday and my cell phone is turned off. Over the last few months, I've hardly left it on. I only call back if work calls me.

Mom and Dad are visiting a church friend and the house is cold. Empty.

I try to type out an outline to the story I had told to Travis months ago, but I end up staring into my computer screen at a blank Word document that shrouds my room in white. The words I've typed look strange and out of place. It's as though I've chosen every wrong word in a sentence. I quit without saving.

I go downstairs and check Mom's medicine cabinet for anything to make me feel like I'm not a failure at writing.

Can someone fail at what they love? If so, how does one cope with it normally?

The cabinet is empty. No drugs to take me away.

Life is easy now. Wake up, go to work, repeat. Don't rinse. Just repeat.

The fridge is the same. Empty. No alcohol.

I scrounge around for an Adderall and take one for the hell of it.

I wander the Internet, clicking random sites, trying my best to kill time. I want time to just be dead. Every passing minute is a minute I could be doing something with my life.

It's agonizing to watch your life go by. Minute by fucking minute. A life without a purpose. Without a goal. Without any hope. Now that … that is a dangerous thing.

I type "homemade drugs" into a search engine just for fun.

A quick high. Maybe that's what I need.

I find a page dedicated to a chemical I've never heard of. It's called Dextromethorphan, or DXM for short. I can't even pronounce it. Found in cough syrup, if drank in large quantities, it has the same effect as PCP.

Hell, I don't even know what PCP is.

I check a few sites that have positive reviews of people who have taken it. Doesn't seem too bad. I grab my keys and head for the store. What's the worse that can happen?

⌇

I'm home again, lying on the floor with my back to the fridge, staring at the Safeway bag in front of me.

I felt like a junkie buying it. Correction: I am a junkie.

I stare, not moving. My hands are shaking.

Prescription drugs. Alcohol. Those were all different.

This is serious. This is the real stuff. Hallucinogenic. Dangerous in large quantities. Jesus! I am about to down a bottle of cough syrup to get a high. What is wrong with me?

I twist off the cap, close my eyes, and lift it to my lips. I pause.

The Adderall is doing nothing. I've never felt so calm and shamefully excited at the same time.

Funny how people work. Mom, for example, fell apart the minute she walked past a slot machine. That unknown firework was lit in her brain. And the first thing that exploded was common sense. Self-control.

This is everything I have told myself not to do.

I'm smarter than this. But this is my slot machine. And I don't know where the spark comes from. I wish I did, because once it lights, I can't stop it.

The cough syrup gurgles down my throat.

I really wish I did.

I begin to cough and stagger into the fridge. The syrup spills and gushes out the sides of my mouth—I look like a vampire sinking his teeth into a victim.

I drop the bottle and it clatters on the floor, but doesn't break.

I'm literally coughing up my lung, down on my knees and hands, choking and dry heaving. My eyes burn with tears.

What in God's name have I done?

I start to laugh to make myself not cry.

At least I'm not too far gone.

I still feel guilt slip over me like a cold blanket.

⤳

I'm scared to death now. I've turned off all the lights in the house and have buried myself in blankets in my bed.

Things are starting to move and I think I'm hearing voices. Suddenly, I'm more scared than I've ever been.

I'm trying to count sheep in my head. But one always seems to come up missing.

Maybe I can sleep through the side effects. Wake up tomorrow and this whole mistake will be forgotten.

No harm done.

The original feeling of excitement has long since passed.

I don't want to be high. I don't want to be scared like this.

I want to be a normal kid again.

I get up and plow through Mom's cabinet again. I find what I think are painkillers, grab a few, and head to the bathroom.

I need to sleep. Now. Before the DXM hits me. I can't wait the thirty minutes it takes for these drugs to reach the bloodstream. I take out my keys and try to crush them. It looks easier in the movies. I push down as hard as I can and the pills break into a sloppy powder. I bend down, hold one nostril, and breathe in. I feel like a vacuum sucking up a fine sugar. It burns slightly.

I look up to mirror and notice how tired and worn out I look. I stumble off to bed and I drift into an uneasy sleep.

⌒

My eyes fall open and the walls are alive. They move like snakes, slithering and shifting and turning and rotating.

I let out a muffled scream. *Close your eyes!*

Colors and shapes appear and sift through the dark. It's like my very own Aurora Borealis in my bedroom.

My heart is thumping like a Congo drum, horribly off-rhythm.

I reopen my eyes and the walls keep moving. My table in the corner is growing and shrinking like a beating heart.

I close my eyes again.

This isn't real.

I hear muffled whispers in my ear. Or scratches. Something I can't define.

I plug my ears but they don't dissipate.

I throw my blankets aside and stand.

As a kid, I loved going through the fun houses at the local fair. Mirrored walls, plate-shifting floors—all that cool stuff. It was all so unreal. But you knew it'd disappear the minute you wanted it to. You could run through and end up at the start. Alive and safe and standing again on firm ground.

But this isn't fun. And I can't just run away this time.

My balance has always been good, but right now, I can't help but slam into the purple walls around me. Now they're yellow. Now pink. Purple again.

Tears are trickling down my face along with something else. I rub my nose with the back of my hand and feel wetness. I bring my hand to my eyes and see bright red pulsing everywhere. I'm bleeding.

I've overdosed. I know it.

I start mumbling a prayer. The last time God and I had talked, I slammed a door in His face.

The whimpering dog returns to His master. He's trampled the neighbor's flowers. Barked at, and scared, the neighborhood children. Made an embarrassment out of himself.

The bad dog that is me has come back home with his tail between his legs.

He's sorry.

I'm sorry.

Oh God! I'm suddenly on the floor again, huddled in a ball. Please don't let me die. Please—

I hear whispers again—wordless mumbling oozing from the walls.

I crawl along the carpet and slither into the bathroom. Even with closed eyes, the ground tilts and shakes.

The bathroom's automatic light flicks on and burns me. The light it shoots out dances across the mirror, spots bleeding into the dancing wall.

I splash water on my face. It echoes as if the sink is a large ravine.

I'm on the ground again and don't know how I got here.

Crying.

I'm sorry.

God, please, I'm so sorry.

I keep repeating my words until the automatic light blinks off and I am welcomed into complete darkness.

Chapter 26

The Best Advice (June 2005)

From where I'm sitting, I can see expansive lines of warehouses for miles, as though I am in the middle of a fully dominated Monopoly board. Not including the Humane Society across from me, this pit of Tacoma is all industrial. Paint, plastic, pop, and all other sorts of other manufacturers and distributors set up home here in the serial-killer capital of the world. I sit behind Pepsi's barbwire gates in the break area, literally twiddling my thumbs.

Break area is a nice term for it. Really, all that it consists of are a few dilapidated plastic chairs huddled around a fireplacelike ashtray. Above me is a torn and faded Mountain Dew canopy fluttering in the wind. It's always a sad sight to see when you expect a multibillion-dollar company like Pepsi to provide you with something a little better than this. A break room with a working microwave and air conditioner would be nice. Maybe an ashtray that is emptied instead of collected in a bucket that serves as the conversation pit outside. But I always take my breaks out here, since the inside break room is even worse, complete with sticky floors, stained seats, and God knows what smells leaking out of the closed refrigerator. All the "You're Working at the Best Place on Earth" posters plastered on the walls wouldn't have helped my mood anyway.

So I take my breaks alone, shivering outside in the Washington weather to the rhythm of my thoughts. Nowadays, I prefer a reclusive feel. And today especially, I want to be alone.

My head is fuzzy, a fog still coursing through my veins. I took the DXM over three nights ago and I still feel groggy.

My body moves slowly, my thoughts trailing behind like a tired dog.

I have never done something so dumb. So incredibly terrifying.

It was indeed the newest low point of my life.

I need help.

I can never do that again.

I drink down the first gulp of hot chocolate spit out from the rest-stop coffee machine that is in our lunch room. It wiggles down my throat like a warm slug.

I open my Cheetos bag and begin eating my standard, vending-machine lunch that has, more or less, kept me going here for almost a year now.

I keep my eyes trained on the ground until the back warehouse door pops open.

Kathy is my older, lowest-on-the-chain boss, who dresses as though she lives next to the Goodwill (unlike the other Kathy who I met on my first day of work). Her face is far more wrinkled and worrisome looking than it should naturally be at fifty, and her blonde hair is straggling down her face like an old, cut up rug. It looks like she hasn't had the chance to comb it in years. That, or she doesn't care. She fits perfectly here. Out of my five bosses at Pepsi, she was the lowest on the totem pole and, coincidently, my favorite.

"You on break?" Her voice sounds harsh as she waddles her tiny legs toward me.

"Yeah, but I only have a few minutes left."

"I'll extend it." She pats the stuffed pocket of her jeans. "You want to come with me?"

I laugh. A genuine laugh that is usually hard to produce when I am at work. "Yeah, I'd love to."

"Good." She looks behind her at the camera pointed toward us above the warehouse door. "I don't want those damn cameras to see me and then have Mike bitching at me for starting up again!"

I get up to the sound of my body cracking with discomfort from the abuse of the long weeks I have been putting in at the job. I follow her silently out the back gate as we make our way to the back of the Humane Society building. We stop and stand at the tiny garden that has recently been built and fenced in.

"Is this place sickening or what?"

I simply nod my head.

The garden we are in is the place where the Humane Society workers take the animals, if no one comes to adopt them, for their last playtime before they are put to sleep. Well, that's what we think it is for anyway. A final walk, much like death row, we suspect. Everyone at the warehouse has a morbid way of looking at things, and after a year, that includes me.

Kathy reaches into her pocket and pulls out her pack of cigarettes. She offers one by gesture, but I decline. She pounds the pack into her hand until she is able to produce a single smoke, which she quickly dangles from her lips like a bad Dick Tracy movie. She tucks the pack away.

"You know, you're the only one here besides Christian who knows I still smoke. God, if Mike finds out, he'll be riding my ass the rest of my days here." She lights her cigarette and takes out a third of it in one clean, hard drag.

Must have been some day—

"Can I ask you a question, Nick?"

"Shoot."

Kathy's eyebrows arch. "Why are you still here?"

I take my eyes off the garden and meet hers.

What an odd question to ask out of the blue.

"What do you mean why am I still here?" Without knowing why, I am defensive in my tone. "I'm here for the same reason you're here."

"Money, right?" She inhales deeply.

"Exactly." I smirk, but she doesn't reciprocate.

"You see Nick, that's what I don't quite understand. I'm stuck here and I need the money. You on the other hand, don't."

I almost laugh. Almost.

"How long have you been here? About a year now?" She points her cigarette at me with every sentence.

"Yeah, about that."

"You don't belong here," she says with bitterness in her words.

I want to blurt out a response. Tell her how wrong she is. But a part of me knows she is right.

She continues after her pause. "You see ... Mike, me, Dennis, all of them ... we're all stuck. All of us here got complacent with our lives. You've met all the drivers, all the bosses, all the bigwigs that run this show. They all hate their jobs. But they have ex-wives, kids, mortgages to pay off ...you know what I'm talking about. The money is good here, I won't say nothing about that. But—"

I can't keep my eyes off her. My smile is replaced with a stone face.

She exhales the last of her cigarette into the air, leaning her head back.

"I'd fire you right here and now if I could."

"What?"

She looks me in the eyes. "It kills me to see you here in this hell." She nods her head as though she is saying something she had wanted to say for a while. "You're too bright a bird for this cage. Go back to school. You're too smart to burn out here."

I look away from her, taking my attention to the garden in front of us.

Too bright a bird for this cage. From someone like Kathy, it sounds almost poetic.

"Kathy—"

"Get the hell out of here." She stubs out her cigarette in the dirt before she flicks it without care into the air.

"Don't become me. Please, I'm begging you, Nick. As your boss, that's all I ask of you."

She turns and hobbles away, back injuries from her years of being a Pepsi loader still haunting her. I wait until she disappears into the warehouse before finishing my drink and heading back to work.

Too bright a bird for this cage. It's the only thing I can think about for the rest of the work day.

Chapter 27

A Falling Star (July 2005)

When I enter the kitchen after work, Mom and Dad are sitting at the dinner table, buried underneath a mountain of paperwork. They talk in whispers as I step in.

"Hey. What's going on?" I ask as I open up the nearest cupboard to grab a glass.

Mom's eyes are lighthouses. "Everything went through. They accepted us."

The adoption. I already know about it.

"Yeah," I say, opening up the fridge and pouring out some juice. "I thought they already did that."

"Yes, but they set a date now." She holds up a paper. "We're set to go pick her up. In China. Next month."

I almost drop my drink. I sink into a chair at the dinner table.

"Wait. What?" I don't know what else to say.

"Can you get time off of work at the end of July?"

"How long?" I try to sound happy. I really do.

"We'll only be gone two weeks—"

"And then you'll be a big brother." Dad makes a sad imitation of squinted eyes and laughs.

I don't respond with a laugh. "I can't get two weeks off Mom. They'd kill me."

"Then just one week." She's not demanding it. She's pleading.

"Mom ... this is all ... really ... sudden."

"I know. I know, but we really want you to come. This is a big deal."

She's got one thing right. This is a huge fucking deal.

I'm a mess and I'm definitely in no shape to be a brother. How can I be responsible for a sibling when I can't handle myself?

Mom is better now, that is for sure. But can she handle another kid? Or am I just making excuses because I'm too scared?

All I can do is nod my head. "I'll try."

Mom smiles. Her smile is absolutely gorgeous. "Thank you Nick."

I check my cell phone. Earlier that afternoon, I got a call from my friend Zach, who was back in town from college, inviting me to a nearby party. I told him I didn't feel like going, but now I've changed my mind. I had to get out. Away from this huge change.

"I gotta go. I'll be back later tonight."

I get up and grab my coat and am gone in a matter of seconds. I am a master of running away from things.

My whole life may be a mess. But it is my mess. My problems.

And now, everything is going to change.

⤷

"Who cares if you're drunk? Just drive Nick, okay?" Chantelle shrieks into my ear.

She's right. I don't. Care that is.

Somewhere along the way, I might have, long ago. Back when I was a model student. Back when I was a youth leader. Back when I was the only thing that held my family together. That version of me might have had the ability to say no and gone to sleep right there on the steering wheel instead. I only wish I knew where that version went.

Some future brother I'll be to an orphaned Chinese girl, eh?

I look over at the girl in the passenger's seat. Chantelle sobs. Blood trickles down the side of her head and clumps together in her hair.

The whole night had gone fine up until now. It had been casual. Just another senior party where everyone tried their best to drink away everything they had learned. Funny thing is that I graduated last year. Yet here I am, celebrating someone else's graduation and entrance into college.

It's always someone other than me.

The parent on guard had asked everyone who planned to drive to hand over their keys. Actually, come to think of it, the mother demanded it. At the time she asked, I had so many painkillers coursing through my veins that I could have cared less what she asked of me. I hid my keys and lied to her. Told her I didn't drive. My friends backed me, telling her I was the most responsible person they knew.

The party commenced. I was happy. I had my keys and I drank myself stupid.

And here, hours later, back in my car, my head whirls as Chantelle screams for me to take her home.

"What happened?" I ask.

Her eyes light up. "The bitch hit me is what! God, Jennifer was out of control. She drank so much she couldn't even stand. So I helped her to her bed so she could sleep and then out of the blue, she just started hitting me!" Chantelle's curly black hair flies around as though we are standing on a beach with a warm breeze passing through, but I know it is just a drunken optical illusion.

I also know there is more to the story than she is telling me, but I don't care to know any more than I have to.

"Chantelle." I close my eyes to stop the spinning. "I can't drive. I'm sorry."

"If you don't then I'll go drive my own car. And I'm a lot more messed up then you."

I massage my temples. I don't care about myself anymore, but I can't let her drive. As much as I hate it, it is still me. I am still that codependent asshole.

I sigh and reopen my eyes. "Listen—"

Just then the overhead light bursts on, sending both Chantelle's and my eyes shut; twin vampires shunning the glow. I turn my attention to the backseat, where Zach has opened the door and gotten inside. His massive rugby body sends the car down a notch.

Before I can say anything, he starts shaking his head back and forth. "It's so fucked up in there. Jennifer is having a fit! We got to get out of here before her mom finds out you're driving." He smiles for some reason. His pupils are large and he sniffs as though he has a cold.

God, now he thinks I'm going to drive too—

Zach looks over at Chantelle. "You okay?"

"She's fine," I answer for her.

Zach's dilated pupils meet mine. "Good. Then drive, Nick. Now." He commands.

I turn around and readjust my position on the steering wheel. One hand on the nine position, the other on the three.

The Department of Motor Vehicles calls it stability. I call it trying not to pass out.

I fumble in my pocket for my keys. When I dig them out, they feel unusually cold compared to everything else in the summer night. My eyelids fall shut, whether by my own doing or by the chemicals raging through my bloodstream, I can't tell anymore. Both the alcohol and pain killers are depressants. If I keep my eyes closed any longer, I'll pass out.

I sigh. Screw it. What more do I have to lose?

I turn toward Chantelle who is in the same dreamy state I am in.

Who cares? Right, Chantelle? I'm so far gone it doesn't matter what I do anymore! Right? I want to yell at her.

I answer for her. *Right.*

Nothing matters anymore.

I search my key ring for the car key and slide it into the ignition.

Drunk driving. The one thing in my life I said I would never do under any circumstance.

I laugh. That was before all of this. Before my life became such a mess. But unlike the celebrities of Hollywood, or the friends sitting next to me, I had no turning point that led me over the edge. I have no reason to become what I am now. I don't have a father who beats me. I'm not overprotected. I haven't been peer-pressured into anything.

There is no significant event. Nothing that makes sense anyway. Looking back on everything, nothing seems in chronological order anymore, and everything is very loosely connected, if at all.

I sure as hell can't piece it together. What's the point? Can anyone be the person they used to be after destroying their life?

I manage to open my eyes. After releasing a sharp snicker, I twist the key.

I have done all of this to myself, and there is no way back.

The engine roars in the summer night.

Chapter 28

Broken

A moment later, I turn the ignition off.

"I'm sorry. I can't do this." I glance over to Chantelle, who is now cleaning the blood off her forehead with her sleeves. I give her a shrug.

"Nick, you either drive or I'm getting out and driving my own ass home."

I look back to Zach for support. His head is sunk back. He looks dead.

I try my best to keep my own head up and eyes open.

"I won't drive. But I won't let you drive either," I say.

The overhead light is blinding and, before I know what is happening, Chantelle is already stumbling out of my car. I shove my door open and find myself hanging half outside of my car.

"Chantelle!"

I can hear the scratch of her car keys against paint. I guess I'm not the only one who lied about their keys.

"Chantelle!" I scream. "You can't drive like this!"

"Fuck you, Nick! I can do whatever I want!" She rips open her car door and falls in. After the slam, the night is quiet, except for the slow, steady bass of the music from the house we left from with such class.

I slide back into my seat and rest my head on the steering wheel.

"Oh God. What do I do now? This is all my fault."

Like an annoying mosquito, the overhead light wakes me off of the steering wheel.

"Thank you, Chante—" I stop.

It's Zach, his reanimated body moving fluidly into my passenger seat.

"We going or what?" he asks.

I want to punch him. "No Zach, we're not. I'm not moving a fucking inch."

His nose sniffles and his body shakes, but still he is able to catch my eyes with his. Even in his state, he must see that I'm not joking.

"Whoa, Nick, calm down, man. We'll be fine, just drive slow." His smile is crooked. "It's easy."

"No."

Getting drunk and stoned is one thing. That's my life now, but it only hurts me. No one else is involved in my downfall. Drunk driving is something completely different. It is the number one thing on all the lists I had ever made in school of things I would never, will never, do.

"Listen. I need to get out of here. If Jennifer's mom calls the cops— well, let's just say I can't be caught drinking underage again."

I laugh. "So I'll get screwed instead if we get pulled over?" I can tell the alcohol is talking in sync with my thoughts.

His fist slams into my dash, sending the car rocking back and forth. "You either drive or I get out of this car and have Chantelle take me home. And I bet she's legally blind with how messed up she is."

He lets his words soak in.

"You decide. But do it fast." He opens the door and gets out.

Oh God.

I turn and look to where Chantelle's car used to be.

Actually, it hasn't moved. She is probably passed out on the steering wheel.

I turn my attention back to Zach.

"Wait."

Zach bends down.

I have no choice.

"Fuck you, Zach, for putting me in this situation."

The lesser of two evils, right? At least I'm not as drunk as her, right?

My head is swirling.

Right?

"Get in."

He does. I start the ignition again. Before putting it in gear, I look to Chantelle's car. Now, it is nowhere to be seen.

Please God, be with her.

I roll down my window to let the air flow. My eyes feel like sinking weights. The road in front of me tilts back and forth like when I was a child, spinning around the living room for minutes on end in circles and then trying to walk.

I am no child now. And this isn't my living room.

The trees and houses sway in an invisible wind. I glance over at Zach who now seems to be half in a coma. I hope my dose of Adderall this morning left some trace of speed in my system, even though it is well beyond the effective hours. I lean my head as close to the windshield as I can get it. I can feel the chilled glass even without touching it.

I take Zach's strung-out advice and go slow down the large hill connecting Bonney Lake and rustic Sumner, below in the valley. I make my best effort to stay within the speed limit, though half the time I try and remember the speed limits from previous drives since the signs are just blurry numbers that I can't make out now.

Driving between the yellow lines is a game of drunken Operation. Hit the curb and hear the buzzer. I'd have lost the game turns and turns ago if that were the case.

Somehow though, I make it to Zach's house, pull into his driveway, and cut the engine.

"Zach!" I shake his gigantic shoulder; the size of my entire frame. "Wake up, man. We're here."

His body jerks. "What? Where?"

"Your house."

His head smacks into the window before I can react.

I get out and fumble toward the passenger side door. A part of him is still conscious, so moving him isn't as hard as I think it will be. He holds most of his body weight while I struggle to hold the other.

We make a slow trek to his door.

"Thanks, buddy." His sloppy grin reappears.

"Do you have keys to get inside?" I ask.

"Yeah." He jingles his keys and laughs.

"Do you need any help getting to bed?"

He hugs me. "No man, you're a good friend."

"Good night, Zach."

I let him lean on me until he finds his keys and cracks open his door. I leave in silence.

Back in my car, I sit staring off into the waving trees surrounding his house. What the fuck did I just do? I just risked his life and everyone else who drove past us. I put everyone in danger.

I close my eyes and feel sick.

Who am I?

I open my car door and puke in his driveway. I hold onto the door tight and feel my throat burn and tears streak down my face.

After I am done, I wipe my mouth on my sleeve and close the door. I turn the key once again. Ironic. I can sleep right here until morning. There are no screaming, drunken friends yelling at me to do so. It is just me with no pressure. But I have to get home, away from this nightmare. I am this snowball rolling down the hill, collecting more debris on the way, turning faster and faster and—

I take the wheel and make my way home, swerving down the street.

I feel sorry for any child that gets me as a brother.

I'm a good kid doing something I promised never to do. A large part of me wants to get pulled over. I deserve it.

But I make it home intact.

I tumble up the stairs to my room, tripping on a step that sends me slamming into the wall. I recover and continue up. Once inside my room, I close the door and fall into my bed. I smother myself in blankets. My whole world feels like a freefall.

When I was a child, I used to cover my entire head with blankets because I was afraid of the dark. Now, I cover my head as shame rocks me sleep.

Chapter 29

Half a World Away (August 2005)

We fly to Beijing and I leave all my drugs behind. Hopefully, I can repeat Europe and cold turkey everything.

I get the window seat on the plane, away from my parents, and drift in and out of sleep.

I haven't gone without some sort of medication in me for less than half a day in two straight years. It's pathetic how weak my body feels without them; as though without the poison my body can't function.

My metaphor is horrible, but I'm tired and my thoughts lag along with the plane ride.

When we land, God knows how many hours later, we meet our guide, Fay, who is the representative of the company, Faith International, that does all the in-between work for adopting families. There's a whole crowd of other parents and families tailing her for the same reason—a tour group of baby hunters.

Outside the airport, we all gather into a fancy tour bus like the ones used by American rock stars.

Memories may be wonderful, but withdrawal symptoms sure aren't.

I sleep the entire way to the hotel; in the heartland of this unknown country.

The hotel is huge; hundreds of rooms smooched together. A hotel whose only purpose for being is to house the adoption business. We meet hundreds of people from around the world. Every single room is booked with a waiting family. It's disgusting in a way, but I feel a great respect that so many people from so many cultures are gathering to get these kids out.

It's endearing.

Fay tells the group that we won't meet the babies until later in the week. Until then, we are to be carted around China to sightsee. Climb The Great Wall, visit a few black markets and jade shops.

It's odd until I figure out the reasoning behind it. They make deals with companies to cart our American dollars through shops. Nothing says money like parents wanting to make a lasting memory of the place where their adopted child was born.

The first night at the hotel is the worst. I toss and turn in the hard bed, getting up and pacing the hotel almost hourly. No matter what hour it is, there are always people around, moving and swaying like a busy ocean.

Only this ocean is anything but calm.

Chapter 30

Air-Conditioned Ignorance

The overhead PA system crackles as Fay's tiny voice whispers through the tour bus. Her English is quite good for having been born in China, but then again, I don't doubt for a second that she has probably done this hundreds of times.

An official baby seller. A trafficker of souls.

Some job title, eh?

As she has done with countless other soon-to-be parents, she starts to talk about the history of the cities we pass. It is her job after all. I can only make out a few of her words since most of her voice is gobbled up by the roaring engine and hum of the air conditioner vent above my head.

I should have sat up closer.

The bus shakes as we barrel down the gravel road toward The Great Wall. This is one of our first stops on the tour.

I'm not complaining.

Outside the bus, it must be at least ninety degrees, but my teeth bite down on my lips to stop from chattering. Cold sweat leaks down my shirt. I'm two days clean, and that makes me happy, even though my body is in the middle of a nuclear meltdown.

I take pauses from writing in my journal and watch the landscape scroll by my window. Outside in the fields it is so hot from the relentless sun that I can actually see the air vibrate along the ground like gasoline vapors snaking up into the sky. The land is completely flat, save for some mountains off on the horizon.

The air is cleaner here than in Beijing. Here, I can see for miles without the trademark Chinese smog blocking the view. Everything is green, with farmlands dominating every direction. Men and women with the stereotypical pointy hats that protect them from the sun work in the field.

The faces of the workers are grim. Emotionless. They turn and watch our luxurious bus coast by.

I don't know why, but I try to wave to one of the workers. It is the only thing I feel can connect me to a world where the language barrier is almost impenetrable.

They don't wave back.

We pass a small town. Tiny brown houses litter the main road in clusters, crumbling down to nothing.

Turn away, I tell myself.

But I can't.

Every apartment building is dilapidated, every window broken out, and the streams are no longer clean; the water swirling into a grayish-brown mess along the sides of the street.

How can a country that is a superpower fall so far behind? How can they live with themselves, ignoring the basic human rights of their own people?

This is not Beijing. There are no tourist traps. No ads or black markets.

This isn't Europe. Nothing is glamorous about this.

My life's problems are nothing compared to this.

This is the real world behind the mask of business.

I turn away, ready to write down every detail of the things I can see, but the roads are so sloppy that my scribbling becomes illegible.

I look up once more and catch the eyes of a worker, a man whose hands are stained with dirt. His stare is the most solemn I have ever seen. It is not of anger, or even sadness, or even pity. It is a stare of absolute nothingness, and it scares the hell out of me.

I turn back to my journal and attempt, once more, to scribble madly for page after page so I don't have to look up again and see eyes like that.

I fiddle with my throw-away camera that has only two shots left.

Damn. Why did I waste so many pictures on Beijing when a place like this needed to be photographed and looked at the most?

I place my camera back into my day bag. Maybe it is best not to remember this place. I also put away my journal. Now more than ever, I am not in the mood to write.

I try to listen to Fay over the speakers instead, but I still can't make out a single word. The hum of the air conditioner keeping us all nice and comfortable is too loud.

Chapter 31

The Great Wall of China

My foot misses the next misshapen step and I tumble into a sea of people, who, like dominos, smash into the stone wall one by one. Through my heavy breathing I struggle out a sorry. I receive a stream of different dialects I can't understand. The crowd marches on as I put my back to the wall and try my best to control my heart rate.

Looking down the rolling valley, I can see the wall stretch like a snake into the distance until the smog swallows it up. Funny how The Great Wall of China can be seen from space, but when you are actually climbing it, the pollution of the ever-increasing factories nearby blurs the view after only a few miles.

Like there aren't enough damn child-labor factories already over here.

From what I can see, the steps resemble something out of the Tower of Babel. Not only do I have to crane my neck up to manage the near vertical stairs, but every step is unique in size. Every step is different from the last. A Slinky wouldn't make it one step down this thing.

The recently installed guard rails, misplaced looking as they are, help, but the constant flow of people ascending and descending the same route make it almost impossible to get a firm grip. Or even a grip at all really.

My breathing is returning to normal.

I had challenged Dad a race to the top over two hours ago, but with this godforsaken path, who knew which of us was winning. I make my feet continue up the stairs.

I pass a group of Italians. One of them, a small boy, smiles up at me.

I must look like a mess. I am drenched in sweat from the sun, and being off of Adderall for almost a week isn't helping. But beyond the headaches, the shakes, and everything in between, I have never felt better.

I pause in my steps. "*Ciao!*" My pronunciation of "hello" is horrible, but I don't expect any better from trying to teach myself from an *Italian for Dummies* book for fun one summer.

The child laughs. "*Ciao. Sei Americano?*"

I nod my head. "*Ciao!*" I stretch out my hand and recite some of the only phrases I can remember. "*É bella!*" I say, telling the boy how beautiful the view is.

"*Come ti chiami?*"

I try to respond, but all that comes out is a long laugh. He joins in with me. He's hit the depth of my Italian knowledge and knows it.

"Good-bye," he says in rough English.

I nod and go back to my trek up the stairs.

I smile as I climb. This is a once-in-a-lifetime experience.

I shake my head as a walk, laughing underneath my breath. Here I am, climbing one of the Seven Wonders of the World. A week ago I was drugged up, driving drunk, and twisting off bottle caps for a living, and now … now here I was, on top of the world where, all clichés aside, I feel I can see everything clearly for the first time. I am being given the chance to step away from every problem I have created for myself over the last couple of years so that I can observe them from afar. For once, things are beginning to make sense.

It's the best feeling in the world—to understand life. Even if it is only for a borrowed moment.

I take in a deep breath. Sometimes you have to wake up first in order to dream.

Beads of sweat trickle down my back. Every group of fellow climbers speaks another language. Spanish, Dutch, Chinese, dialects from Africa. It feels like an international pilgrimage to the top of the world for … what?

God, whatever we are all hiking toward, there had better be a bar there—

I reach a flat area consisting only of an empty guard tower. I hobble inside the shell of what used to be something magnificent, but is now concrete flakes and graffiti.

"Nice shirt, mate."

I turn to see a tiny, smiling, mustached face.

I look down at my *Price Is Right* T-shirt. I didn't think anyone in China would ever recognize it.

"Thanks."

"You from the States?" asks the man who looks like the Monopoly guy, minus the fancy top hat and cane.

I lean on a wall and let my T-shirt soak into the cool concrete.

"Yep. From Washington. Not the capital, the other one."

"Right." The short man extends his hand. "Name's Hank." His grasp is firm. "I'm from Sydney. You want to continue up with me? We've almost conquered her!"

I laugh. "Sure, I honestly didn't think it'd be as hard as it is."

His laughter, along with his body, disappears into the summer sun outside.

I curse myself for not buying sunglasses.

I follow. Our way up is as slow as it had been before. This isn't Boy Scout camp. It is every man's legs for themselves. Hank stays in front of me since the staircase is only wide enough for two, maybe three, bodies.

"So what are you doing up here?" Hank asks, as we reach an area of clearing.

Conversation with strangers is nothing new for me. Back when Mom was in the hospitals, I had to make due with talking to random people who loved to initiate pointless conversations.

Nod and agree. That is the key.

"Uh, well, my parents are here to adopt a little Chinese girl." Hank turns around and grabs my shoulder. He does it so fast and unexpectedly, I almost let out a small scream. "Well congrats, mate! The big brother, aye? Excited?"

"To tell you the truth, I don't really know what to think of it all."

Hank turns and continues up. After another ten feet, he becomes a walking chatterbox.

"Well, I admire your parents then. And you. Takes a lot of heart to adopt a child. Especially from here of all places. These kids need to get out of this communist pit so badly." He tilts his head as he climbs. "You and your parents came with a group I take it?"

"Yeah." I laugh at the absurdity of how much this stranger seems to know. "How'd you know?"

"That's how it works. Groups come here, take the grand tour. You know, go to all those jade and silk slave-labor factories where everything's real cheap. They do that so they can make some quick profit off the Americans before they even get the kid."

The guy is straight on the mark; and sadly so.

"Why'd your parents want to adopt in the first place?"

I grunt as the steps wind suddenly.

I know the answer, but how do you go about telling someone that your mother doesn't remember you growing up? That seventy or so electroshock therapies had almost completely fried her long-term memory? How can I explain that my mom wants another baby so that, this time, she can remember her child's youth?

"Not a clue." I'm a world away from my life, but I still find it easier to sideline the question.

"Why are you here?" I ask.

"Me?" He grins. "I'm traveling—" His sentence trails off as we make our way up the last of some difficult steps and reach another clearing. We dive for shade. The sun above us is becoming almost unbearable.

"Water?" He takes off his backpack and offers his water bottle to me.

"If you don't mind—" I grab it from his hand and let it flow like a river down my throat. I don't even pause to breathe. I easily drop the contents of the bottle by half. A Pepsi-made water has never tasted so good. Hank smiles as I hand back what is left inside.

"So, just here to travel then?"

He takes a gulp of water and looks me over.

"A mate of mine from Sydney, a lawyer type, saved up as much money as he could to buy this brand-new 2005 Mercedes. Cost a fortune. More than thirty thousand! Well, he saved the money and bought it. Told me it was the best money he'd ever spent."

I don't have a clue what he's talking about.

I nod and agree.

I drove a shitty car with locks that were busted, thanks to my many locked-my-keys-in-the-car-again stunts. The windows didn't roll down and it frequently died in the middle of highways, but it drove. What I wouldn't give, though, to have a nice, properly working car—

"I envied him for that." Hank takes another swig from his bottle and wipes the sweat from his forehead. "So I gathered up the cash to get a similar car. I saved up about twenty-seven thousand or so, walked into the dealership, signed half the papers, and—" For the first time since meeting him, Hank has stopped smiling. "I walked away."

"Walked away? You didn't get the car?"

"Someone once told me that money could never buy you happiness.

That it could never replace experiences. I walked out of there with the best feeling I've ever had."

I wait for him to stop his movie-style dramatic pauses.

"My friend was wrong, you see? I walked out of there, bought a ticket to Amsterdam and have spent the last year and half traversing the globe. I've been everywhere from climbing the Alps to climbing The Great Wall of China." He smiles. "I realized, and am still realizing, that seeing this world and meeting people such as yourself is what is important. Life experiences, Nick. That's what the best money I ever spent is going toward. Not a dumb car."

I don't nod and agree. I don't know what to say to such a speech from someone I have just met. His passion is oozing out of him and I can feel myself choking out a response.

People are like this in movies. Not real life. "That's amazing ... so ... commendable. You're a smart guy, Hank."

"Commendable? Nah, not at all." Hank sweeps his hand in front of him as though brushing away the comment. "Kind of selfish, really. What you and your family are doing by getting that girl out of here, and into a family that will actually love her—"

He puts his hand on my shoulder. It doesn't feel awkward at all.

"Now that is commendable. Your family is commendable." He nods. "But enough with the sap, you ready for the final stretch mate?"

I smile. "Yeah. Yeah I am."

⌒

His shirt is drenched, as though he has fallen into a horrible Chinese tsunami on the climb up, but his smile is bright enough to compete with the sun. Dad looks as though he is a man who is on top of the world. He is soon to be a father again and, at fifty years old, he has beaten his teenage son to the top of The Great Wall of China. It makes the old man prouder than I've seen in a long time.

Hank and I weave our way through the maze of camera-poised tourists, avoiding the dead ends of flashing cameras and grouped families. I have never heard the word "cheese" so many times in so many different languages.

Dad is shaking hands with another soon-to-be father from the group we traveled with named Roy. Roy is barely in his mid-twenties and, by the looks of it, he is ready to hike the whole wall again, just for fun. He is the comedian of the trip, with a pocket full of balloons to blow up and mold for any Chinese child lucky enough to get near him. My parents are by far the oldest couple of the entire group.

"We got up just before you," Dad pants out. His eyes don't move from the view.

No picture I take there can describe the vastness. The hills roll for what seems like forever, disappearing beyond human eyesight into the smog. Everything looks so fake and static, like looking at some large city from an airplane window. It's surreal to feel so removed from modern society, yet be in one of the most populated nations in the world.

"Now … now I've seen it all." Hank laughs and puts his hand over his eyes to block out the sun that seems closer than ever.

Dad notices Hank and takes his camera out from the fanny pack I always make fun of him for wearing.

"Can you take a picture of us?"

Roy offers his camera up. "Mine too?"

"Sure!" The three of us situate ourselves at the edge of the wall.

"Ready? Smile!" Hank hollers a beastlike roar to signify that we have indeed made it up the entire way—made it to the top of the world.

Dad roars next.

I can't control myself and begin laughing as the camera flashes. It is a large belly laugh that shakes my entire body.

I am away from everything. The drugs. The alcohol. My job.

Hank takes another shot with Roy's camera.

I am still laughing.

He hands the cameras back and offers his hand to me. "Best of luck to you mate! You've got an amazing road ahead of you."

"Thanks, Hank." I shake his powerful hand, for once, with equal intensity.

He turns to leave.

"Hey, maybe we'll meet again like this," I call out to him.

"I don't know. My two years are up—"

"Says you or your money?" I yell.

"The money is out. I'm not," he says and evaporates into the crowd.

Chapter 32

Born Again

"This is it, Mom."

She shakes her head. "Yep, this is it alright." I expect her to be nervous, but her words come out strong.

I smile and look outside the tour bus window.

China is fascinating. The streets we blaze past are a messy collage of clashing technologies. BMWs honk their way through traffic. Millions of women on old, rusty bikes try to balance buckets on their free arm as they swerve around the cars. Donkeys plow their way through the crowds at a gallop, pulling large carts of food and boxes. I have yet to see a crosswalk. Or speed limit signs. Or even lanes for that matter.

The bus plows through a group of pedestrians who magically part just in the nick of time. We barrel down a side street, the bus rocking as we hit every patch of rough dirt that hides between the gaps of broken concrete in the road.

The houses on our side are small and hutlike, scrunched together to make it look like a line of a few dozen replicas of the Bates Motel.

I sigh.

No more pictures on my throw-away camera. I use the horrible camera on my cell phone instead. Then again, even if I had more pictures to take, would I still want pictures of this? Do I really want to remember this?

The bus comes to a sudden halt. I look over to see an assortment of high-rise buildings. They look ugly and gray. Out of place.

The lot next to this particular high-rise is a wasteland.

The dusty ground can't be seen. I imagine that the rubble and chaos are what make up the floors of the huts here. The people that reside here, the people that call this home, are living their lives on trash.

In America, we have dumps for our garbage. Here, the ground is the dump—right next to these rich, lush towers where babies are sold.

It's not the wasteland that is ugly here.

In fact, it's downright beautiful next to these towers.

We file off the bus and soak in the humid, smoggy air.

We follow Fay down a broken street. No one in the group says a word. A nervous tension competes with the smog.

A tension of realization—of becoming parents, or guardians, or grandparents, or, in my case, of becoming a brother.

Fay lines us up and we enter the building in single file, one family at a time.

This is neither fancy nor glamorous. This is a black market for babies.

We stomp up the stairs where a gruff looking Chinese man motions us down a plain, but oddly crooked, hallway.

They gather us like cattle into a small, even plainer, empty room.

Fay addresses all of us like a speaker at a rally.

"This is it! We wait here. They call you out family by family to pay the rest of the fee. Afterwards, we all meet in adjoining room and you meet your child."

She smiles. A real, gorgeous smile. A smile that counters everything negative in the building. It outshines the horribleness of the barred-up windows, the peeling wallpaper. Her smile screams: Thank you for getting these kids out of here.

The group livens up after the somber walk.

Everyone beams.

Smiles. Smiles. Smiles.

Had I ever seen a real smile before this?

I feel like a genuine hero.

～

"Rogen," the stout man calls out from the doorway.

Mom and Dad get up.

"Do you want to come with us?" Mom asks me.

"No, I'm okay here. Thanks."

They follow the man inside.

I take out my journal from my backpack and start to scribble and take in my surroundings.

The writer in me comes out in moments like this. Places like this are fuel.

Somehow, I have to incorporate all of this into a story.

What a crowd we are in! A crowd willing to spend thousands and travel across continents for these lost children.

Across from me are Roy and his wife. All the children from the other families crowd around Roy. He's charismatic with his Robin Hood good looks. He's taken out his balloons, bending them into impossible shapes (a bike, a kitty, a heart) at the request of the shouting children.

I wonder: What are he and his wife here for? My first thought is that they can't conceive on their own.

Roy's laughter bounces and infects these children. His love for children is undeniable. Boundless.

To his side, his wife holds a bottle of Jack Daniels, a present for the head of the orphanage. He had requested either a bottle of Jack Daniels or a carton of cigarettes from each family. A gift to show your appreciation that he was "gracious" enough to let you take one of their children.

Love. It sure as hell isn't here without these adoptive parents.

I look over to the corner of the room at another future parent. I can't remember his name, but I can't forget his face. It's pudgy and large. He used to be a football coach. Permanent lines of stress are etched into his skin from screaming plays to scared junior high kids. His eyes are large and beady, and his hair, when seen, is forever stuck in "hat-hair" position.

The Sports Father is rattling off to his wife about the current state of the U.S. economy. His wife is polite and nods along to his words.

I've been told before that people chatter when they're really nervous. If that is true, then this Sports Father is terrified.

I can see he is just like Roy. He may have put on a mask, but he is here for the same reason. He is tough. Man-of-the-house tough. He was going to become a hero and doesn't even know it.

I look around and continue to scribble away.

I haven't met many of the rest of the group.

There's the family of five who has adopted three times before this trip. Unlike the Sports Father and his family, the wife of this brood is the king. Her husband, sitting nearby, is quiet and reserved. She, on the other hand, is hard looking and talks with slow, steady words. She reminds me of a feisty Italian; laying the law down. The woman who spanks her kids and makes sure their hands are clean before they eat.

But in this toughness, there is love.

I close the journal and tuck it back into my bag.

Love.

It is the reason we were all here. All these diverse parents have this common trait, and this trait will save at least a few of these children.

My parents are back.

They aren't talking.

Why are they adopting? Dad is along for the ride, and I think it is Mom's way of laughing in the face of Fate.

"Ha!" she'd yell in Fate's cringed face. "I beat you!"

She can't remember my youth. Or the time I bit her wrestling. Or the time I dangled dead rats over the strawberries we picked in a field near our house just to gross her out. Her illness and all the electroshock therapies have taken away all those moments in time. A forced Alzheimer's.

But this little girl. She'll be able to remember everything about her. Every moment. It makes me happy that she has another chance.

Even I am excited. I may be a terrible excuse for a brother, but, hey, at least I am trying.

If I only knew that the girl in the other room screaming would be the key to the redemption I had been searching for all these years.

⌣

"So what happened?" I throw my arms around Mom who then takes the seat next to me on the wall. The Chinese man continues down the list of family names.

Mom chuckles and shakes her head. "Just like a black market."

Dad pipes in. "They took us to this small room, where we sat down and laid out the deposit on the table."

The deposit. The price of a child. The price of a life. Over four thousand American dollars.

"The guy sitting in the executive chair across from us said nothing. Just went through every bill, one by one, with a magnifying glass." Dad's arms dance around in disbelief of what just happened.

"No way!"

He nods.

"So did you give him our gift?" I say with a smirk.

"Yeah, but they just threw it into a large pile in the corner of the room with all the other gifts. He probably didn't like that we didn't get him alcohol."

I love Dad.

"Wait until he sees that the only thing that's in that big bag is a snazzy Boeing pen and tin of cheap chocolates."

All three of us crack up.

❧

It's a little over forty minutes before everyone is done paying and are all herded into an even smaller room across the hallway.

Roy is silent, and it's the first time I've seen him this way. He looks more tired then he did after climbing the wall.

The Sports Father is chattering faster than the Chinese do.

The woman with three kids is no longer issuing orders.

Dad sets up the camera. Mom waits.

Fay comes in and tells us the order in which we'll receive the children.

We're third in line.

Everyone stands as a mess of small bodies smother in through the door.

Roy finds me in the crowd.

"Hey Nick, can you take pictures when we get her?"

"Yeah, Roy. No problem. It'd be my pleasure." He hands me his camera and pats me on the shoulder. "Thanks Nick. We're first."

I follow. The Chinese bodies that just poured in form a half-ring in the adjoining room. A women shuffling papers stands in the middle. It looks like a baptism being rehearsed.

The woman calls out Roy's last name in a rough translation.

The couple moves from the crowd and walk into the ring's center.

A string of men holding crying babies enters the room.

Dear God.

It's like nothing I've ever seen before.

A conveyor belt of kids. Like candy. Like they're nothing but money in diapers.

I click a picture. The delay of a digital camera is something I'm not used to from dealing with my cheap throwaways, and by the time it goes off, Roy's wife is already holding the baby in her arms.

They pose for me.

The woman calling out names does not wait for this picture-perfect moment to occur, however. She has babies to sell. She immediately calls out the next family.

They crowd in. I end up taking pictures of someone's backside.

It's a mess of crying now. Babies everywhere.

Before I know what's happening, Roy has his camera back and I'm beside my parents. Roy is filming on the side with our camcorder. They plop a baby in Mom's arms.

Mom frowns.

"This … this isn't the right child."

The woman calling out the next family stops in mid-sentence. She shuffles through her paperwork, her eyes narrowing and alternating glances between the baby in Mom's arms and the clipboard. She turns her head and spouts something in Chinese to the men behind her.

A man appears with another baby in hand. He replaces the baby in Mom's arms.

I'm speechless.

We're pushed aside and are in seats at the back of the room in a matter of a few seconds.

Dad is holding the child now. He's crying.

I look over to the Sports Father. As he rocks the child in his massive arms, tears are exploding off his cheeks with every belly laugh that escapes him.

It's a horrible place, and a horrendous, faceless procedure, but right now, this room is full of joy. Full of hope.

"Do you want to hold Noel?" Dads asks.

Noel. What a beautiful name.

I say no.

I can't hold her.

She's delicate and soft. Among grownups and children alike, she's the only one in the room who isn't crying. Her large eyes watch us in curiosity.

"No," I repeat. She needs to be held by someone worthy. Someone who is not a mess. She needs to be held by strong arms and mine are much too weak.

I touch her forehead though.

She's absolutely gorgeous.

My baby sister.

Noel.

Chapter 33

New Sister, Aisle Nine

Okay Nick, all you have to do is just breathe in.

I inhale.

It's not as bad as it looks.

I exhale.

So, I'm standing in the middle of a billion Chinese people in a foreign Wal-Mart. I begin to push my way through the chattering sea of black hair.

I have a baby in my arms—

I rock Noel again, but it doesn't stop her ten-month old lungs from practicing her higher notes. Her screams rip through the air.

A screaming, scared baby.

I pull her closer.

Have I ever even held a kid before?

I hold her awkwardly. I'm positive I've never even touched a child before now.

I scan the crowd for anyone I might have known from the adoption group. I stop in my tracks.

How about that. Lost in a Chinese Wal-Mart. Maybe they were on the second floor? Back in the States, even a one-story Wal-Mart is hard to handle. This one has three stories.

Fay had the group stop in at the store after visiting the orphanage to pick up anything we had neglected to bring along. Mom gave Noel to me even though I protested. We only had twenty minutes before the bus took off again, and the only way we were going to get everything we needed was to split up.

Again, I don't know why they entrusted me with the kid.

"Excuse m—" I let my sentence get sucked into the collage of untranslatable Mandarin.

I look at Noel. Her brown eyes are large, her head still flat on the bottom where she'd been forced to lie in a crib all day, ignored by the orphanage mothers. She stops crying, and in its place comes a tiny whimper that sends her lip shivering up and down from cry withdrawal.

"I'm sorry, kiddo, I have no idea where to go."

Why my parents have assigned me Noel *and* the task to go find diapers is beyond any logic I can wrap my head around.

I push my way through the aisles of brand names I can't pronounce. I pass the meat department where open bins of mysterious animal parts are being grabbed for by a multitude of hands.

Where the hell will I find diapers if I can't even tell what any of the products are?

Again, I breathe in.

I can do this. Just stay calm.

I am pushed into a candy aisle, much as I can tell, and am amazed at the prices. To the American dollar, an entire package is the same price as a single bar in the States. Communism at its very best.

As I make my way through the crowd, I am hit hard from behind by a rogue shopping cart, which unlike its American cousin, can go in any direction without directing the front. I turn to a small woman who blurts out a jumble of words to me. All I can make out is the "*dui bu qi*" that means "sorry." I keep wading my way through the crowd.

I am stopped by a family of four, who strangely look too much alike. The husband smiles and holds his camera up.

"Picture," he says.

I smile. "Okay."

Tall, orange-haired teenager with an oddly held Chinese baby, looking so confused by his surroundings that it seems as though he has had a lobotomy—nothing strange here to take a picture of!

The father motions his kids to flank my sides. Before I am told to smile, I hear the click and am blinded by the flash. They all laugh in unison and blend back into the human sea of short bodies.

I gotta get out here. Now.

I ride the peculiar, flat escalator up, watching a hundred eyes bear down on me from the opposite side.

I make my way through the clothing aisle, hoping I can catch a member of the adoption group that I had seen go to this section earlier.

Finally, I recognize a familiar face.

"Fay!" I nearly scream her name.

She runs over to me with wide eyes. "Ah, Nick!" She says in rough English. "I said only have twenty minute here. Where are your parents?"

"I lost them trying to find the diaper aisle." I laugh at the absurdity of the situation.

She smiles. "Come. Follow."

For the head of an international adoption program, Fay may be small and frail looking, but she moves like a bat out of hell and tramps a straight path right to the exit.

As I follow Fay's charging rhino imitation, I try to compare this situation to when I had been lost in Venice for a day back when we all went to Europe. I can't see a connection. There, I had found some American tourists to help me out, and I was able to figure out the basics of the language after a while. Here though, I feel completely and utterly lost.

At a Chinese Wal-Mart with a new sister in hand, I feel my old life, which seems so distant now, sifting slowly away.

It is the best high I've ever had.

Chapter 34

A Promise I Hope I Can Keep

We've only been back in our hotel room for twenty minutes before Fay knocks on our door and requests that my parents come with her to sign more legal documents.

More documents. There were so many documents to read, and fill out, and sign, it often seemed like you were buying a house, not adopting another human being.

"Can you watch Noel?" Mom asks.

I stop writing in my journal and set it on the table next to me. I sink into the seat and look to Noel. She is sitting on the bed, staring at all of us. She hasn't moved an inch since we got back. Nor has she made so much as a whimper.

She must be scared out of her mind. A whole new life is nothing short of terrifying.

I can relate.

"Uh, well," I stammer out. Taking Noel through an insane obstacle course in a Chinese Wal-Mart was one thing—

"We'll only be gone for a little bit, and she's tired. You can put her down to sleep." Mom walks over to Noel and picks her up like a small cat, propping her up against her shoulder. She rocks back and forth.

"See," she says, "It's easy."

I sigh. "Alright."

Mom smiles and walks over to me. I stand up from the couch and hold out my arms. Noel is so light, that it feels like Mom rolls air into my arms. I place her on my shoulder. I'm no expert, but I'm getting better.

"Just rock her for a little bit and then put her in the crib." Mom leaves with Dad.

All at once, the room is oddly noisy. The buzz of the muted television showing a Chinese newscast is louder than usual. It mixes with the distant wailing of other babies in the hotel. I doubt that an entire hotel full of new parents and scared children can ever be quiet.

"How you doing Noel?"

It's the first time I've used her name. Up until now, I've always called her Kid or The Baby or some other ridiculous thing.

Her skin is soft and delicate, like I'm holding fancy china instead of a baby girl. I lean her off of my shoulder and place her on my forearm. I've seen new mothers do this. Or maybe it was Mother Mary in a painting I saw of Jesus being born. I don't know.

I begin to rock my upper body, standing in place in the middle of room.

"Some day, eh?"

Her frame shift in my arms as she snuggles her head into my hand. She's growing so tired that her eyelids blink like Morse code.

"My name is Nick. I don't think I actually told you that."

She blinks and squirms in response.

"I'm your older brother."

Your mess of an older brother, that is.

I close my eyes and feel her heartbeat pulse into my arm. It beats at a jack rabbit's pace.

I continue to sway.

"I have a lot of growing up to do, Noel." I continue my monologue. I heard somewhere that talking to babies soothes them. But what do I know? "A lot of growing up to do. I'm still not perfect … but I'm trying."

Her heartbeat is steady now. I open my eyes. Her eyes are closed.

"God help me I promise I'm going to try my best." I'm whispering now.

I walk over to the crib and set her inside. The joints shake and squeak. They've probably held millions of babies before her. A million scared kids, with equally scared parents in the bed next to it.

I kiss her on the cheek.

I walk over to my bed and sit on it for a few minutes. I stare off through the window. Our hotel is situated on the edge of some river, but the view is nothing spectacular. Across the river are factories of high-rising smokestacks; blinking lights barely visible in the smog. I'm sure the famous London fog has got nothing on this place.

I grab my backpack and unzip it, taking out two odd-shaped bottles. One for each hand. I hold them out and sigh.

Over the past week, I've felt better than I have in my entire life, but skeletons in the closest never really seem to disappear. Travis is right about that. It looks like the skeletons in my closet have traveled with me.

I bought the bottles in street markets for, literally, nothing. The brown liquid inside taunts me.

I place them back into my bag, wrapping them up in my extra shirts. I take a glance back to Noel.

How long I can pretend to be the strong brother? The good son? The role model everyone thinks I am?

I crawl underneath my covers.

I wonder how long I can keep the demons at bay.

Chapter 35

Dollar Value

The city of Beijing is bustling with life the moment I step outside the hotel. China is always busy, but now the streets resemble a midday parade in Times Square.

I begin at a steady pace toward the lights and music coming from the east. This is my last night here and I want to soak in the last of the sights and, of course, hit up at least one local bar before the end of the night. It's been a long week without Adderall or Clorazapam and I want to reward myself.

I made a promise to Noel and I'm not about to break it only a day later. I am going to make sure I only have one. Just one drink and that is it.

My parents went with Noel to Guanjo to stay a week more, with more sightseeing plans to fulfill and papers to sign. I would have loved to stay, but I am flying out tomorrow to get back to Pepsi. I promised Mike I'd only be gone a week, and no matter how life changing it is here, and no matter how horrible Pepsi is to go back to, I don't want Ian and Christian continuing to cover for my absence.

As I get closer to the main square, everything becomes massive. Larger-than-life billboards litter the sides of every building; synchronized light shows of advertisements that go too fast for me to understand. The street slowly turns into one giant sidewalk. It is one of the first places where I haven't seen a car. Crowds flow in every direction like a fairground. Kids on modified rollerblades that swirl with neon lights skate to American pop music that blares from the speakers of nearby record shops. I pass by a few of the shops and notice they have movies that are still in the theater or not even out yet. Many of the descriptions of the movies are misspelled or list the wrong actors and directors.

Hell, I can do a better job forging these!

Everything is weird and wonderful. Like a daydream. Among such business and noise, I am so calm and collected.

I stop in front of a large group of old women who are dancing to a nearby boom box. The dance is slow and formal. As in real graceful dancing, not something you see in today's clubs. It is like watching an old black and white film. There's something strangely hypnotic about it.

My eyes catch one woman in particular in the back of the third line. She is so small and fragile looking, I can't keep my eyes off her. I don't put it past her to be in her late seventies. Her moves are slower than the rest of the women, yet they still hold an ancient grace I've never seen before. Her arms and legs twist to a different kind of rhythm than the others, something I can't hear through the noise of the street.

Here I am in a country devoured by poverty, ruled by a communist government who only cares about money; a government that once allowed their female children to be killed off because their population went skyrocketing. But here, this woman is dancing as if she doesn't live in country with such a dark past. She is at peace with the world around her. In America, her family would have had her in a rest home by now.

I fiddle in my pocket and take out the fifty U.S. dollars I shoved into my pockets earlier that morning. In China, since minimum wage is nonexistent and money is scarce, it is considered a huge gesture of kindness to give out one-dollar bills to people who help you. A dollar to them means so much more than I always took it for. To me, it means something to waste on the dollar menu at some fast-food joint, but to them, it means survival.

I approach the old woman and hold a dollar out to her.

"I want you to have this," I say, knowing she doesn't understand English.

Her head tilts to me. Her eyes light up and a smile whips across her face. She rips the bill out of my hand and lets loose with a flurry of Chinese words that make no sense. She talks with such swiftness, such intensity, I think she's having a panic attack.

I smile, nod, and begin to turn away.

It feels good to—

I feel a hand tighten on my shoulder. I snap back around. She holds up her crooked index finger telling me to wait. She turns and scuttles off into the crowd of dancers where a small backpack is lying on the ground. She crouches over the bag and begins digging as though the scent of a bone is driving her wild.

I gulp. *Oh God. Did I offend her?*

I stand motionless for what seems like hours.

She's going to kill me and then sell my kidneys on the black market—

Her hunched-over body comes into full view as she makes her way back to me. Her hands are cupped together, shrouding whatever it is she found. She speaks again and I nod my head back and forth, hoping she will understand that I haven't a clue as to what she is saying. She nods to my hands.

I hold them out and fear she can see them shaking.

As she places her hands into mine, her wrinkly skin feels cool against my own. Her hands shake with excitement as she removes them.

There sits a zipped-locked bag, with a cherry, some grapes, seeds, and a walnut.

At first, I look up in confusion. She smiles, but it looks forced and sad.

"I can't accept this," I say.

She folds my hands together and returns to where she was standing when I had first noticed her. With closed eyes, she starts up her dance once again.

I open my hands.

This is everything she has. Everything she owns. A single dollar made this woman give me her prized possessions. With only a dollar, I changed this woman's life.

I put the bag in my pocket and turn back toward the hotel.

I should be happy. I should be overjoyed that I brought someone so much happiness. But I'm not.

My whole life feels like a charade. A lie. I make people think I have the answers, when in truth I know absolutely nothing.

Soon I'll be back home. Back to the mess I've left. I am no one to look up to.

The urge to go back to my hotel room and drink myself stupid only confirms my character weakness even more.

The more people trust me, the more people look up to me, the angrier I get. The more I wish they'd realize I am not the person to follow.

I am never destined to be a hero.

Chapter 36

Drink It Up

I am halfway through the bottle of sake before I take a break. It is the most disgusting alcohol I have ever had, and the only thing I can afford as a chaser is an equally horrible-tasting Chinese pop from the hotel lobby. I switch on the television to combat the silence.

Tomorrow I am going to be hitching a ride with Fay's husband to the airport. Until then, I am staying at the hotel for the night. My parents and Noel are probably far into Guanjo by now, signing more legal documents and touring the rest of the country. They still have a week left. I have to get back to the States and get back to work.

I laugh bitterly at the thought. Here I am, on the trip of a lifetime, leaving early on account of my entry-level job that I hate with a passion.

Mike told me that I could stay however long I needed to, but I told him I didn't want to screw anyone over.

No matter how much I hate the job, I still can't shake my codependent habits. I always have to make everyone happy.

I take another shot and shudder.

I rotate the strange-looking bottle in my hands. It is only a quarter past nine according to the universal clock on the bed stand.

Why am I still doing this to myself? After everything that has happened, why?

I put the bottle on the table, get up, and search through my backpack that is sprawled on the other twin-size bed. It is packed full, the zipper almost popping from its track. When the zipper finally gives slack, everything inside spills out like a dam burst. I grab a small Chinese box and take out the two beautiful jade figurines inside. They are ice smooth, perfected by slave labor. Earlier this week, the adoption group had made a mandatory stop at a jade factory. I was so close to the workers, I could smell the sweat off their brows.

Next, I take out the various bottles of alcohol I bought over the last week; one bottle of sake and two oddly named vodkas. I place them gently, side by side, on the bed. I dig through my clothes to see if there are any more.

There aren't.

I toss the clothes to the other bed; little knick knacks from The Great Wall flying out with them.

I dig through my empty backpack and at the very bottom, tucked away, I find what I am looking for. It is the small, zip-locked bag. I open it with great care; something that I had not shown the rest of my belongings.

I let the contents of the bag fall into my open hand. The cherry is now squished, red seeping out like blood onto my hands. The walnut is still in intact. No cracks. The hard grapes are also just as she had them given me.

I am crying. I attempt to hold back the tears, but I'm unable to stop their flow. The tears burn my eyes and drip down my cheeks like rain.

"This isn't me," I tell the room. "I can't break my promise. I can't live like this anymore."

I put everything back into the small bag and tuck it away back into the backpack. I grab all the bottles of alcohol and make my way to the bathroom. The automatic lights turn on as I fall in front of the bathtub. I take the first bottle of sake and pop open the cork. The air instantly smells of the rice wine. I hold it above the bathtub, ready to tip it over.

I can't do it.

My arm is shaking.

The devil and angel are on my shoulders. The halo and the horns argue like a cliché cartoon.

To tell the truth, I am my own devil.

I tell myself that I don't have to do this.

The angel on the other shoulder doesn't say a word.

It flashes memories of people through my head.

Grandma. Kathy. Dennis. Travis. The mysterious Fourth of July kid. The dancing woman. Dad and Mom.

All these people look up to me.

Admire me.

Believe in me.

To them, I am the writer I always dreamed of being. I am the son to look up to. I am the worker who is dependable. To them, I am everything I don't allow myself to believe.

I tip the bottle.

They say you're your own worst critic. Give whoever said that a medal, because they were spot on.

But even the worst critics can still be fired.

The green liquid gurgles out, creating a swirling tornado down the drain.

I struggle out a laugh. After all this time, it seems so simple a task to rid myself of such a complex problem.

When all three bottles are empty, I head back to the table in front of the television, grab the half-drunken bottle of sake, and pour it out as well.

The bathroom garbage is filled to the top with empty bottles. I go back and lie on my bed. I turn my phone on and flip through all the grainy pictures I have taken with it over the last week. I stop scrolling when the first picture I have ever taken of Noel pops up on the screen.

When we got her at the orphanage, I took over fifty shots with my camera phone. It was a moment I never wanted to forget. I put the phone away and tuck myself under the covers.

Maybe I'm not a hero, but I'm sure not going to be the villain either.

Chapter 37

A Mentor Appears (January 2006)

Life is a funny thing. It seems as though it often likes to repeat itself.

I'm walking down a row of offices, scanning the nameplates on the doors. This time though, I'm not looking for Mr. Brown and this is no longer high school.

I am a college boy now.

The first thing I did when I got back from China months ago was apply at a local community college. I may still work at Pepsi, but I have a goal now.

I've lasted a whole quarter so far.

I am proud of that.

I stop at the corner office. This is it.

Lori.

She is my new English teacher this quarter, not a guidance counselor.

This time I am prepared to not shun advice. I am here to seek it.

The first day of class with Lori was unlike anything I had ever experienced before. She had a wild look about her. A middle-aged woman with a fire in her eyes. The intensity and passion she radiated was, simply put, nothing short of scary. The first lesson dealt with writing down childhood memories of our neighborhood. She radiated undiminished, untouched, pure optimism. It was refreshing to see.

She was, for me, Robin Williams from *Dead Poets Society* after only one class session.

Following her class, I went home with an almost possessed feeling, and dug up the old, half-written manuscripts in my closet; including the one that I had once pitched to Travis and given up on shortly thereafter.

I knock and hold my breath.

Anyone that has the power to convince me to write again is someone I need to pursue.

The door opens to reveal a smiling teacher.

"Hi, I'm Nick from your English class," I blurt out.

"I know!" she chirps and backs up. "Come in, come in."

The office is plain with two additional cubicles that house other teachers. She leads me to the corner where I sit down across from her.

She folds her hands on her lap. "What can I do for you, Nick?"

I shift my eyes around the room. My leg is thumping up and down. I haven't been this nervous since going to the ADD doctor years ago.

"I really don't know how to word this. I'm not sucking up, but—"

I look her in the eyes. My heart is killing me, but her warm eyes help me ignore it.

"Your class yesterday was nothing short of amazing. You teach with such … passion. Like nobody I have ever seen. I can tell you love what you do."

Lori was a writer with two books under her belt. I had never met an author before.

I had always been the one to look up to, but I never actually had someone to look up to myself.

"And—" I stutter.

And now I have someone to admire.

I dig through my bag, pull out a dusty stack of papers, and place them gently on her desk.

"I was wondering if you could help me. I used to be a writer."

"Used to be?" she asks.

I sigh. I have never been good at asking for help, but I let my guard down.

We talk for nearly an hour.

I pour out my heart to this woman I've just met.

I don't know how, but somewhere between China and now, the walls that I have so carefully constructed over the years are crumbling down.

I tell her how I have wanted to be a writer since I was a kid, but somewhere along the way, I compromised that dream. I tell her about how I shoved it aside and the faith that I once had in myself disappeared in a blur of substance abuse. How the half-assed manuscripts I tried to write just gathered dust in my closest. How seeing an actual author with such love for their career lit a fire in me. I tell her everything I can about where I think I might have gone wrong. How I lost my dream.

Simply put, she made me find the part of me that still wanted to be a writer, even after I thought I had buried the idea in a grave.

At the end of our talk, she is happier than when I first came in.

"Nick, I will gladly read this."

"Are you sure?"

"It'd be my pleasure." She pulls the stack toward her.

"Thanks Lori." I get up and leave.

"Nick?"

I turn around.

She holds up my papers. "This is the first step in becoming a writer."

I smile at my newly found mentor. The door closes gently on my way out.

Chapter 38

One Rainy Day (February 2006)

The rain is relentless.

It moves like a whip in the wind, slicing in every direction, knives from all sides beating down on me. The raincoat Pepsi has provided me to work outside in is little more than a yellow tarp.

You'd think that a gigantic and legendary corporation would have paid more to keep their employees happier than this.

Because, right now? I'm drowning.

All afternoon, the tiny Pepsi trucks have rolled through the barbwire fence, with my job being to count their inventory and put away, stack, and wrap all their empty shells.

Today, I decide not to use gloves. It's raining so violently, I doubt any urine will still be stuck on the shells.

In between trucks, I warm my hands inside the warehouse by twisting more bottle caps. My mind wanders like a lost child.

What an odd world.

I have a new, beautiful sister. I am going to college. I am trying my best to completely cut alcohol and drugs out of my life. And I am going to Lori's office almost daily to go over my writing and ideas for novels.

Yet, here I am, still at Pepsi. Still at this horrible job.

I've been outside over an hour now and the rain seems endless.

Mike has just clocked out early and he stands in the doorway to address me, zipping up his own heavy, Pepsi-issued coat.

"Good job, Nick!" He grins.

"Thanks," I say and feel water spill into my mouth.

"Keep working like this and you'll have my job in no time!"

He walks to his car, the hood of his coat protecting the hair that he doesn't have from the rain.

By the time his car disappears down the street, another truck has backed in.

I continue to wrap and stack hundreds of shells.

This is my life.

Out of the truck comes a man in the same coat as Mike. His hair is graying and his mustache is clean and trimmed. Dark circles are under his eyes. He is probably just finishing a fourteen-hour shift.

Dally smiles over at me. "Livin' the dream, you and I."

I can't help but join him in his smile.

Truck drivers are an odd band of people. Some swear like sailors, while others are constant church-goers. The only common thread amongst them all is their hatred for their job.

Oscar Wilde once wrote, "All of us are in the gutter, but some of us are looking at the stars."

Smart guy, but he must have lived somewhere where he had a clear sky to look at every night. Here, the factories bleed smoke into the sky. There may be stars beyond the haze, but we sure as hell can't see them from here.

Dally starts unlocking his bay doors, throwing them up to reveal hundreds of various products, and, of course, more shells.

I begin to help him pull the empty shells out of his trucks onto the stacks I've already made.

"Where's Ian at?" Dally asks.

"Up front. Checking the other trucks in. It's more work."

He laughs, but the rain drowns it out quickly.

"That may very well be true, but at least it's inside." Dally stops in his place and raises his hand.

"Dennis!"

I look behind me.

Dennis stands where Mike had been minutes ago.

He's tired. His eyes are sagging. What's left of his hair is frizzled like a clown. He walks toward us with a curve in his back. He doesn't even bother to put on his patched-up coat.

It may be miserable out here, it may be raining as though it were some biblical flood all over again, and it may sound like the dumbest thing, but Dennis's smile is bright enough to counter everything.

He pats me on the back and shakes Dally's hand.

"I haven't seen you in ages Dennis!"

"Morning shift. I rarely work this late." He looks over to me. "I hear you're finally going to school."

Dally looks over at me. "About damn time."

Dennis grabs my shoulder. "Good to hear. One step closer to getting out of here."

He turns and walks with Dally, who continues to unload his truck.

I continue stacking, trying to listen to their conversation. The wind and rain make it impossible.

After a few minutes, I see Dennis waving at both of us from outside the fence.

His clunker of a car rattles into the night.

I duck back inside the warehouse and grab my inventory sheet. When I walk back outside to count what's left on the truck, I have to press down hard with my pen to combat the weather, but the rain is like a dry-erase marker on everything I try to write.

"Poor guy." Dally is looking out into the parking lot. "I really feel sorry for him."

"Twenty-five, twenty-six," I stop counting and look to Dally. It's raining even heavier now, and his body has become a featureless shape in the downpour. I make my way closer to him.

"Who?" I ask.

"Dennis." Dally grunts and throws down a stack of expired two-liter pop onto a pallet nearby.

"How come?"

"How come!" The rain is nothing compared to the surprise in his booming voice. "Because he's the most generous man I've ever known, and it breaks my heart that he's a complete fucking mess."

Since the ink on the paper is bleeding a river down my clipboard, I only pretend to keep counting.

Dennis? A wreck?

"What do you mean?"

Dennis is so happy. So cheerful. So adamant about pushing me out of here to pursue a better career. How can someone like that be a wreck?

"He's been here thirty-five years. Since he was eighteen. Why do you think he's still here? On a forklift and not in some fancy office with a heater and a roof over his head?"

"He likes it?"

"Right!" Dally motions a bottle in his hand. "He's a drinker. A real heavy one at that. Hell, he's had so many DUIs, I'm surprised they even still allow him to drive."

It suddenly feels colder.

Dennis is like me. Living a double life. An expert at the art of pretending.

"His wife left him and got his kids to go against him." Dally shakes his head. "Man, he's got some beautiful kids … and they won't even speak with him."

Water drips into my eyes.

"But … he's—"

I've stopped pretending my pointless counting.

"I know. The best man you've known. It's a shame. Won't let anyone help him either. I swear he's going to kill himself one of these days if he keeps it up. I just wish he'd get some help." Dally continues to rip the expired pop out of his truck. "The nicest guy," he mutters.

Dally leaves a few minutes later, wishing me a good night and telling me to take a hot shower when I get home.

I stand motionless in the rain.

My head is underwater.

Dennis.

My lungs are full to the brim.

Poor Dennis. A mirror of me. Encouraging others while destroying himself.

I've had a lot of bad days in my life, but standing in the rain now, drowning, is the worst I've ever felt.

⌇

Borders Books is surprisingly quiet for such a stormy and miserable night. I don't even bother to take off my yellow raincoat. I'm drenched and rain is still dripping down my cheeks.

I stand in the middle of the store and unwrinkle a soaked piece of paper from my wallet.

Read Steinbeck, *Cannery Row*, the paper says.

Lori told me to read it. She said it would do me good. I often told her how much I hated my job and being stuck there. She told me I would enjoy this book. That it would be something I'd be able to relate to.

I track down the last copy with ease.

I often think I know the store better then its employees.

This is my second home. Books are friends that I don't have to put on a charade in front of. I don't always have to joke to make it look like I am alright.

I flip to the first page in the book.

"Cannery Row in Monterey in California is a poem, a stink, a grating noise, a quality of light, a tone, a habit, a nostalgia, a dream." I scan the first paragraph. "Its inhabitants are, as the man once said, 'whores, pimps, gamblers, and sons of bitches,' by which he meant Everybody."

I turn to the back flap and read a quote about the book being a funny and bitter commentary on the bareness of existence, about the men stuck in the factories and warehouses they so hated.

It sounds like a good read.

As I make my way to the checkout line, I notice a bright and new sign atop a computer.

"Apply Now!"

Having no paper, I write the URL on the back cover of the book.

What the hell, right?

Before all the drugs and alcohol, before all that, I had tried to apply here, but never got a callback.

I buy the book and head home. I'm in a miserable mood. The news of Dennis hits me harder than I originally thought. I end up taking a spare Clorazapam that I find in my room.

When the fog reaches my mind, I look to the back cover of *Cannery Row* and type in the web address. I fill out the online application, almost quitting several times.

The drugs aren't making me feel better. The rain must have flooded my skull.

I am a waste of talent—a loser who puts his job experience as twisting off caps of expired soda.

Man, if that doesn't scream "Hire me!" I don't know what does.

I fill out the entire form and go to bed in a worse mood than when I was working.

Two days later, I get called back for an interview.

Chapter 39

Quitting the Dream

I hold my time card above the sliding strip and close my eyes.

This is it. I'm finally getting out of here.

I slide it through and, for once, am pleased to hear the beep that follows.

It will be the last beep I'll ever have to endure from this God-awful place. I smile and place my timecard back into its slot.

When I turn to head up the stairs, Dennis drives his forklift over and stops just a few feet from me. He leaps off with a spunk I would never suspect from a man who, straight out of high school, has been forklifting for thirty-five years. Out of everything at Pepsi, Dennis's smile is the highlight. In the movies, when eyes twinkle and faces light up, it seems corny and unrealistic, as though it took the camera crew hours to adjust the lighting for it to happen just so. But when Dennis does it, it feels real. He has that charm.

"Last day, eh?" He rubs his beard.

"Yep." I laugh.

He holds out his hand and shakes mine. This is a man I respect.

"I'm happy for you, Nick." He shakes hard. "Getting out of this fucking place once and for all. You said you were going to school right?"

"Well, yeah, it's a community college, but—"

"Doesn't matter. You were never meant for this place. Not with that mind of yours." He lets go and points at my head. "So what finally lit the fire under your ass to do something with your life?"

"Going to China mostly. I saw things a lot clearer when I was there. And having a sister now—" I sigh. "It's brought a lot of perspective to how I'm going about making decisions. And I got a job selling books."

"No more bottle twisting for you! Nothing brings change like responsibility. Going all the way over to China got you away from this place so that you were able to see what the world has to offer ... and what you have to offer the world. You'll have a remarkable life outside of here. Mark my words. I'm so glad you discovered what potential you have."

Dennis never says much, but when he does, he gets his point across.

"Thank you, Dennis. I can't thank you enough for your encouragement."

"Well, if you ever write that book of yours. I want a first edition. Signed."

I laugh. "Alright."

Dennis gives me a hug. At Pepsi, I have never even seen someone so much as shake a hand.

"Keep in touch, my friend," he says and gets back on his forklift. He smiles, drives off, and is gone.

"I'm going to miss you Dennis," I say to an empty aisle. And with that, I ascend the staircase.

"Hey, Mike." I stand at Mike's door as he looks away from two of the night loaders sitting across from him. They are all laughing at a conversation that dies the minute they all see me.

"So this is it, then?" he asks.

I take a seat next to his desk, facing his side.

"This is it," I respond.

He sighs and swivels his chair toward me. The two night loaders fall quiet.

"You can keep your badge and gate card. You have two weeks to change your mind before payroll takes you off permanently. I mean, you quit once—" His eyebrows arch up along with his grin.

"I'm not coming back, Mike."

One of the night loaders laughs. "They all come back sooner or later."

"Not me."

Mike leans in his chair and folds his arms behind his head.

And here comes the guilt trip. What a great boss.

"So I heard from Kathy you got a new job at a bookstore." He shrugs his shoulders. "I mean, it makes sense, you're into writing and books and all that stuff. But what's this new job going to be paying you?"

I can feel my blood rising. I know what he is trying to do. Everything always has something to do with money.

"A little under eight dollars an hour."

The room goes off in a uniform howl. "That's barely above minimum wage! You're going to take nearly a three dollar pay cut! And for what?"

I want to tell him that I won't hate my new job. That the job at the bookstore is something I've always wanted. I won't despise my life and take drugs to get through my days. I won't have to be complacent. I won't have to—

I could have gone on for hours about the benefits of quitting, but he already knew every single reason.

"Money has nothing to do with why I'm quitting," I tell him. I make sure to use the word quitting and not leaving.

The comment is like a knife to his heart. He shifts uncomfortably in his chair.

I have never been more comfortable in my life.

"So let me get this straight," he says as he massages his temples and rubs his shiny head. "You're taking a minimum wage job and going to school for … what is it you are going for again?"

"English. I want to be a writer."

"English," he repeats.

I put my head down. I don't like this personal angle.

"So, what, you'll make barely enough to live on if you're lucky? That's if you even publish something." The two loaders join in with his laughter.

I join in and they all stop.

"Yeah." I look him straight in the eyes, something I have never been able to do in my year and a half here. "You got it all right, Mike. And you want to know why?"

I don't leave enough time for his sharp wit to answer.

"Because I don't want to end up like you."

I let the words ooze into the fan above us and spread over the office like confetti that gets caught in your hair.

"I don't want to go to school for my English degree like you did, but then drop out because you found better money elsewhere. And I certainly won't work at a job I hate just because the paychecks are nice. Money will never buy my happiness. I want to be happy with my life without compromising. You want to know the most important lesson I've learned here Mike?"

I swear his face is made of stone.

"I may have ruined my life working here. But you know what? It was damn worth it. I realize now who I don't want to be. Who I never want to become. I don't want to become my boss who compromised his dreams for money." I slam my badge on his table.

"I'll become a writer and you'll never see me again. I promise you that." I get up to silence. "Good-bye Mike."

His face is slack, mouth dropped open as though it were dislocated. The offices are still quiet when the door closes behind me.

I walk out with more than just my last paycheck in my pocket. I walk out with integrity.

Chapter 40

A Smile in the Darkness

The screaming is relentless.

I roll back and forth in my bed, contorting my body so my pillows can cover both my ears. But it does nothing to help. Noel's banshee yell pierces the cushions as easily as it has bypassed two closed doors and a spacious hallway. I stretch onto my back and stare at the ceiling in dismay.

I let out a laugh into the dark. It feels like a game sometimes. The "who will give up first and go rock her to sleep?" game. Since we got Noel six months ago, I have become a master at the waiting game. It seems Mom or Dad lose every time and get up with mutters under their breath and bloodshot eyes.

Tonight is different though. I am tired and her wall-defying yell holds no promise of stopping any time soon. My sigh is loud. My parents aren't budging.

It is their way of telling me it is my turn.

"Okay, okay. I'm coming Noel." I slip from my bed into the night's coolness and put on some crumpled pants and a T-shirt. The Pepsi clock I took when I left has its arms wrapping past three in the morning.

Good Lord Almighty—

I pull my door open and cross the hall. The screaming intensifies with every step. When I enter her room, I can see her tiny body thrashing and wailing back and forth inside the crib.

"Noel, its okay, I'm here now." I tell her. I close the door behind me. She stops screaming, but her body keeps swaying with constant gasps for breath. I stand over the crib and reach out my arms. I take hold of her small body and lift her to my shoulder. Her pajamas are drenched in sweat.

"Oh, Noel—"

She rests her head on my shoulder and her crying all but stops. Her body now moves up and down with contorted breathing. I am surprised she hasn't passed out by now.

I stroke her head and back as I pace the room. The indent on the back of her head still feels smooth—she must have laid in that orphanage bed all day.

I walk from one end of the room to the other so many times that I am able to close my eyes without fear of running into a wall or stepping on some nasty, sharp toy.

The house is silent and all that can be heard is the slight whirl of the air purifier's motor, a machine we bought to block out the white noise of the night. I can feel her heart beating softly, almost in turn with her slow, rhythmic breaths. I align my breathing with hers. She breathes in, I suck in air. She breathes out, I do the same. We are one.

Six months ago, I was in the same house, half passed out and praying to God that I could stop myself from self-destructing.

And now—

"How could someone in their right mind abandon you at a doorstep?" I whisper to her ear.

Now nothing is the same.

I feel the gentle push of tears from beneath my eyelids. They scroll down my cheek.

"I want to tell you a story Noel, about why we chose you. Now your Mom, you see, doesn't believe that God tells us to do things. She believes in randomness. That nothing happens for a reason. But one day, when Mom was driving, she felt like she heard a voice from God telling her to adopt you. We all thought she was crazy. Well, crazier.

But she truly believed it was a message. So she set up the meetings, the trip, the location … everything. And now here we are. And to be honest, I truly believe Mom was right. I just want you to know that you are loved—" I swallow hard. "And you will never be like you were in China. Ever"

I struggle out a sigh.

"I can't explain it and it seems so cliché … but everything changed the minute I held you. You're my little sister and I'm your big brother that you'll look up to. And I'm sorry I'm such a mess Noel. I'm so sorry I'm not the role model I should be."

I can barely control my words now.

"But you know what? I'm so blessed. No matter what has happened. If I had a flux capacitor"—I laugh at my own lame *Back to the Future* reference—"and could go back in time and change everything I've done … had the chance to do the right things. If I had that chance, I would give it away. I wouldn't change a single thing."

I never really did find out what pushed me off the tracks all those years ago. But suddenly, pacing Noel's pink room, everything makes sense.

Everything I had gone through had been puzzle pieces of my life and the problem all this time was that I had no idea what the larger picture would be once they fit. I could see the larger picture now. I could see the purpose. Everything made sense in this moment.

"I made you a promise. And I've realized what I'm here to do. I know my purpose. And that promise I made to you … through hell and back—"

My heart is going to explode.

"I'll be here. Clean and sober. A brother worthy to look up to."

I choke out a dry laugh. "If your life is as broken and beautiful as mine is, you'll have a wonderful life."

I rock her, tightening my grip.

"You saved me, Noel. And you don't even know it."

I keep walking late into the morning, until Noel controls my own crying and our breathing, once again, becomes one.

Chapter 41

The Bookstore Life (March 2006)

"Hello?"

I look up from my register and smile at the older woman across the counter

"Hi. Did you find everything okay?"

"I'm looking for a couple of books—" she digs through her pockets until she's able to produce a crinkled-up checklist.

"Ah!" she says, her tiny eyes grow with excitement.

She hands me the list.

"Oh, you want to take this to the customer service desk in the middle of the store." I tell her.

"But I want you to help me."

Huh?

I look over to my co-worker and tell her I'll be right back.

I look down at the list. "Well, you've got easy ones!" I motion the woman to follow. "Follow me and lets us see what we can track down."

The DSM. *The Diagnostic and Statistical Manual of Mental Disorders.*

An Unquiet Mind by Kay Redfield Jamison.

Darkness Visible by William Styron.

Psychology books. I know every single title on her list down to the word. They were books I had checked out at the library to better understand Mom and why she was the way she was.

This is my dream job.

I bounce to the section and excuse myself through a group of customers gathered in front of the self-help area. The woman hobbles behind me.

"Sorry," I say, "all of us walk really fast here."

"No," she smiles, "I just walk slow."

I stare at her smile for a moment. Her eyes look dead and, for some reason, they remind of Mom's.

I bend down to the psychology section, tilt my head, and scan the alphabet. The older woman stays behind me and says nothing.

"Sometimes, these get out of order and it's almost impossible to … ah! Here we are!" I hand over the hefty DSM and plop it into her hands.

"Oh, and here's the other one … and—" My finger slides down the spines. "And the last one on your list. All great choices I must say!"

She smiles again; an awkward, sad smile. She looks tired and frail.

I want to continue talking with her to see why the books interest her, but I can tell she isn't in the mood to talk much.

"Anything else I can do for you?" I ask her from my crouched position.

"No, no thank you, Nick," she says, reading my name off the nametag dangling from my neck.

I smile, stand, and tell her to have a wonderful day.

I head back to the registers, but am stopped halfway.

"Actually, Nick." I turn to see the older woman again. "There's one more thing. I wanted to say thank you for the last time."

Oh please don't let it be another crazy customer.

I'm sure my face shows my surprise.

Her face scrunches up. "You don't remember me, do you?"

I squint. Sometimes, I go through a couple hundred transactions a day. There's no way I can remember every face.

I shake my head and am honest. "I'm really sorry, ma'am, I don't. I apologize." I feel like an ass.

"It's alright." She smiles again. But this time, her eyes do the same. "I came up to the registers a few weeks ago ... and I was crying."

My stomach turns. Oh no. I barely remember what she's talking about. This could end up being really bad. I have learned quickly that, in retail, there are a lot of crazy customers—

"I was having a real horrible day. As you rang me up, you saw all the psychology books I was getting on depression, suicide ... that sort of thing."

Her tired eyes are trained on me like a vulture circling prey.

"And you started talking about how your Mom went through the same thing. Talked about how she got through it. How hard it was. I told you I had the same diagnosis. And you asked me how I was feeling. How I was doing."

She pauses.

"Nobody had ever asked me that before. No one had ever just wondered how I was doing. And I was a complete stranger to you. Then you wrote down a list of different drugs you knew of that could, maybe, give me some help. You gave me advice on how to cope with some of the thoughts I was having. And you told me that everything would be alright. That I should come back often and tell you how I was doing."

My company-provided earpiece shouts into my ear, "We need assistance to customer service if at all pos—" I click off my radio.

"I went home that night, and for the first time in weeks, I didn't have to cry myself to sleep. To be honest with you Nick, I don't think I would have made it through that night without your encouragement and your hope."

I'm shaking. I can't believe what I'm hearing. My legs are sure to fail me at any moment now.

"The next day, I scheduled a visit with my doctor and tried some of the drugs you mentioned."

She sighs. "The name's Mary. I just wanted to thank you. You truly did save me just by caring." She hugs me like a mother does her son. I hug back in shock.

"Thank you, oh God … thank you, Nick," she whispers.

She lets go and smiles—tears dripping down her pudgy cheeks. Wiping them away, she turns and leaves.

I don't bother turning my radio back on to ask the manager on duty for a ten minute break. My fingers shake and it takes me a few times before I punch in the right numbers on the keypad to get into the back offices.

I sit down and drop my head in my hands.

I never take breaks, but—

Just by listening to her. Just for being myself. I saved a woman.

My heart is breaking through my chest. To make an impact on someone like that, so easily, and without even knowing it.

It blows me away.

I always dreamed of working at a bookstore, but never dreamed I'd change lives in the process.

How many people did I need to convince me that *this* is what I was born to do?

Change lives. Help people.

It is in my blood.

I grab a piece of napkin off the lunchroom table and begin scribbling down the experience.

I have the start of an idea … and it might be just crazy enough to work—

Chapter 42

A One-Sided Good-bye

"Heya Nick."

My hand drops the CDs that I'm shelving and I turn.

Ian smiles. That crooked, boyish trademark smile of his.

His bony frame is much too small for his large, blue shirt and pants. Pepsi-issued clothes even had nametags on them now. Like gas station attendants. How quaint.

"Ian!"

I throw my hand out. He shakes it firmly.

"Man, it's good to see you!" I miss Ian. His innocence still reminds me of myself years ago.

I pat him on the shoulder like an estranged uncle at a family reunion.

"Nice place," he says and looks around at the bookshelves with that dazed look of his.

"Yeah, I gotta be honest. It sure is good to be out of Pepsi."

The second I say it, I realize it's a mistake. I pretend to look away and watch for customers who might need help.

There's not a soul around.

I look back at him and suddenly feel sad.

Sad that I got out and he hasn't—like I left a good man to fight a losing battle, alone, in the heart of enemy territory.

To hell with subtlety. Isn't this what friends are for? To tell you the truth of the matter without sugarcoating it? Travis did it for me, and I couldn't have loved him more for doing it.

"Ian, why are you still working there? I thought you were going to school like you said you were going to do?"

His grin is wiped clean off. "I'm a loader now. It's good pay, it's nothing—"

"Whoa." I hold up my hand. "What?"

Loaders make good money, Ian is right about that, but it is the definition of a dead-end job. There is no room for working up, since there is nothing to work up toward. The hours are shit. The people you work with hate their lives—

I suddenly notice the dark circles under Ian's innocent eyes. He must have just gotten off shift—at ten in the morning.

I want to shake him. Scream at him. Tell him that everything Mike says about him being an idiot is true if he continues along the loader path.

In time, his dream of being a sportscaster will easily fade in that place.

Dreams are everything—essential to survival.

I know that more that anyone.

I shake my head. "Ian, please don't tell me—"

"Nick! Chill! Alright? I'm just saving money to go to school."

It's high school all over again. I am Mr. Brown and Ian is the stupid, wayward kid. He is me—digging that damn hole.

"I get paid about fifteen bucks an hour," he continues. "I mean, what do you make here?"

He's trying to prove a point. Mike already tried this and failed.

"Little above minimum wage."

Ian smiles a victory.

"But I'm happy," I add.

His smile twitches, if only for a half a second.

I'm happy. Genuinely drunk *and* sober on happiness.

"Anyway," he changes the subject. "Just thought I'd drop by to say hello and stuff."

"So, is Kathy still there? And Christian and Mike?" I suddenly feel so removed.

The minute I left Pepsi, I decided to never turn back again.

"Mike left to Seattle. Christian got another job. Kathy still is Kathy. Same old."

I shake my head. "See what I mean? Nothing changes there. Everything will always be miserable no matter what they pay you. I'm telling you Ian, get a loan, go to school. Please don't wait, man."

Ian smiles, but it doesn't seem goofy anymore. It's an adult smile.

"Thanks Nick." He looks to his watch. "I gotta get going here. I'm exhausted."

He turns and waves good-bye to me. "Good seeing you."

"You too, Ian."

"Stay in touch. Drop by some time."

He's gone.

"I can't," I whisper to the bookstore.

I can't go back.

Not to Pepsi. Not to my old life.

I can't get sucked back in.

It breaks my heart to wave good-bye to Ian. A friend I can't have. But I am never going to let my old life catch up with me.

Too bad life isn't always fair.

I don't have to fall back into my old life, because it falls back into me.

Chapter 43

The Day Dennis Died

"Can I help whoever's next?" I call out down the register line.

Bookstores don't have fancy flags or blinking lights to call customers to the register. We use a yell more than a whisper.

"Hi! Did you find—," I stop my memorized speech.

There is no need to ask him if he found everything okay. No need to ask if he wants a bag. The older man approaching has no books in his hands.

"Dally." I laugh out his name and shake his hand.

He looks older. His short hair is mixed with more gray than black now. His Inspector Gadget mustache is spotted as well. His face is scruffy and unshaven. It's only been a month since I've seen him, but to be honest, he looks like a wreck.

"Good to see you, Nick." His blue eyes are cold. He briefly looks around. "Hell of a lot better than Pepsi. I knew you could do it."

My smile fades and my Spider-Sense goes on.

Something is very wrong.

"So what's up Dally?"

He bites his lip and his eyebrows sag. "You remember Dennis?"

Of course I do.

Dally doesn't leave room for a response to his rhetorical question. "He died. Last night."

The store seems noisy all of a sudden. The beeps of nearby registers are louder. The ruffle of books and the usually quiet overhead music now hurts my ears.

Dennis?

"What?" I stumble on my simple words. "What happened?"

He gives me a cold look and says nothing.

You know, I can imagine him saying.

Dally runs his hand through his hair.

"I know you've moved on and Pepsi's the last thing you want to think about … but—" He rolls his tongue across his chapped lips.

"Thank you." I take my hands off the glass counter. They're soaked in sweat.

"Funeral's Thursday. Check today's newspaper for all the directions and the time."

"Wow," I finally manage to say.

"I know." He puts his hand on my shoulder. He looks like he wants to say more, but his mouth closes. He turns and walks away.

"Excuse me?" Another customer jumps in front of my register. "No one is at your customer service desk and I need help finding a book."

I want to scream at this woman.

My friend just died! Is your book more fucking important than that?

I want to grab the monitor in front of me and bash it into a million pieces on the floor.

Dead, you asshole!

But I do what I always do.

I pretend everything is fine.

Because it is, isn't it?

"Yeah," I hold back my tears, "follow me."

﹌

I receive a succession of handshakes as I approach the funeral home. The funeral has yet to start, but a thick group of black suits huddle near the entrance doors. As I make my way through the crowd, my eyes meet Kathy's. I nod my head toward her and she attempts a grin back. She looks exactly like I remember her.

This isn't going to be easy.

I say my hellos to the drivers outside, many of whom are still in their Pepsi uniforms, stopping by in between drops because the corporate heads won't let them take a day off. I make my way past the sign-in book, ignore it, and grab a seat.

This is the last place I want to be.

I put my hand in my pocket and fish around until I find the Clorazapam pill.

I've brought it just in case. I roll it in my hands.

It's calling to me. An easy escape. Why do I have to be here *and* suffer? I can just pop the pill and feel wonderful. Absent-minded. Not a care in the world.

I let go of it.

Not now. Not here.

I *need* to be here.

I scan the funeral home. I never wanted to see these people again. Yet here I am, revisiting a life I've left behind.

I sit at the end of an aisle, close to the back. I wait. The front of the room is bare except for a large poster that holds the smile I've missed.

It is Dennis. An older picture of him when he actually had hair! But still, the magnetic smile is there. It may have looked odd to anyone sitting around me, but I smile along with the picture.

Flowers litter the ground in front of the large screen behind the podium—no doubt for a tear-inspiring slide show.

Across the middle of the boomerang-shaped building sits the family. Or at least, what looks like the family. Dally once told me that Dennis had two daughters with an ex-wife. Apparently, he had become a heavy drinker and she divorced him. If rumors were true then even his daughters, who looked only a few years older than me, haven't spoken to him in years.

I bow my head. I definitely do not want to be here.

No matter how fast someone runs, or how far, life always seems to catch up. At least it has with me.

"Heya, Nick." I look up to see a familiar smile.

"Hey, Dally."

He sits down next to me, his blue uniform in strong contrast to the black suits finally starting to file in the front door to take their seats.

"I'm glad you could make it," he says.

"So am I." I keep my head down, not wanting to make eye contact. "That his family over there?"

"Yep. His ex-wife and the kids."

"They know what Dennis died of yet?" I ask, looking up and straightening my back.

Dally's glance at me is brief. "They don't know yet."

I can tell he is lying, but it doesn't really matter how Dennis died. I am here to celebrate his life and thank him for his encouragement. I'm not here to condone his actions.

After that, we say nothing to each other and wait for the room to fill. It takes only a few minutes before the room bulges with muffled coughs and suppressed voices.

Finally, a man in a suit gets up to the podium and introduces himself. He's a reverend, which I find odd since Dennis wasn't the least bit religious. Unless you count being eternally devoted to The Beatles as religious.

The reverend speaks as slowly as someone on death's bed himself. "We are all gathered here today to celebrate the life of a great man. Dennis was a good man, a loving father, a loyal worker, and a wonderful friend." He nods along with several people in the pews. "Many of you know Dennis from his loyal career at Pepsi. Thirty-five years in Tacoma! That's quite a feat, indeed." He pauses. "We're going to start out with a song written by one of Dennis's close friends, David." The reverend steps down and sits in an armchair behind the podium.

An older gentleman from the first row stands up and grabs a saxophone from a nearby stand. He steps into the middle of the room, gives a curt smile, and plays a tune I don't recognize.

Even through the smooth music, I can hear quiet sobs from throughout the crowd. When he stops, he wipes the tears scrolling from his eyes and takes a seat.

The reverend returns to the podium. "And now, here's a tribute to Dennis's life, set to music by his favorite band, The Beatles." Some people laugh, but none sound too happy.

The lights dim. I've never seen a slideshow of someone's life. Thirty pictures from birth to death. It's unsettling in a way. The first pictures are of Dennis as a child, collecting a pool of laughs from the audience. I glance over at his ex-wife. Even she has the hint of an emerging grin on her face.

The next set of pictures travels through the seventies with bell bottoms and peace signs. The eighties introduce his two daughters.

I notice that the farther the slideshow gets, the fewer the people that appear in the photos along with him. By the time the last frame pops up, only Dennis is in the picture.

Isn't it supposed to be the opposite? The older you get, the more people you surround yourself with? Right?

But the last picture is heartbreaking. No wife, no kids, no friends. It is only Dennis, alone in his house. Dally put his head down. I choke back my tears when the music fades and the lights flicker back on.

No one deserves to be alone when they die. No matter what they have done in the past—

Another man comes up to the podium, another friend, who is to read Dennis's sister's speech. I assume it is because she doesn't have the strength to read it herself. At least that's what I hope.

I close my eyes as the speech begins. I shut his voice out and make airspace for my own words.

If you can hear me, thank you, Dennis. Your encouragement meant the world to me. I could care less about what you did wrong in your life. You had two beautiful daughters who you loved even when they gave up on you. I will never forget what you did for me. Without you—

The speaker stops and heads back to his seat. The speech had only lasted about thirty seconds.

The reverend appears once again. "And now is the time for anyone who would like to share a memory to do so." He sits back down.

The silence that follows is overbearing.

A minute goes by and no one stands. I keep rolling the pill in my pocket through my fingers.

I look around. His friends, his co-workers of thirty-five years, even his family, sit still. No one is getting up. My blood thickens.

Was this man so self-destructive that he doesn't deserve a good-bye? I feel like screaming at these lifeless people.

Of course, I don't and, instead, stand up.

I gulp. What the hell am I doing?

"My name is Nick Rogen." To hell with it, I'll say it all. "I probably shouldn't be here, nor should I be the one even talking right now. But this needs to be said. At least by someone. I only knew Dennis for a year and a half at Pepsi. And Dennis ... he's the one who brightened up my days there. Every time I'd see him smile ... that infectious smile of his ... the one that made the world seem better ... he'd ask me how I was doing. And unlike most people, he actually listened. Most people say it out of courtesy. Dennis asked because he truly cared how I was doing." My eyes dart around the room. Not one set of eyes meet with mine.

"He was the one who told me to get out and get an education and continue writing. And I wish I'd listened to him earlier. I wish I had known him longer. But even still, in that little time period I did know him, he changed my life. And I will never forget that beautiful smile. And I pray that none of you do either. Thank you."

I sit down. My whole body, inside and out, is shaking.

It isn't the best speech I've ever given, but it will have to do.

"You did good," Dally whispers and pats my shoulder.

The silence sweeps over the room again, yet this time I swear that everyone can hear my heart beating like mad.

The reverend returns, says some parting words, and ends the ceremony with an invitation to stay for coffee and refreshments in the rear of the building.

I get up and bolt toward the door. I need fresh air. I need to get away. I need to pop a pill and fade away.

An older woman stops me before I am able to escape. Her eyes are glazed over and her black hair is neatly combed to the sides. She smiles at me.

"I'm Dennis's sister."

"Nick," I say.

"Nick, I want to say thank you." She doesn't keep her eyes off mine.

"For what?"

"You said what needed to be said. What wasn't said." She folds her hands in front of her legs.

I hold back my tears.

"And it was beautiful. So, thank you."

I nod my head and say, almost in a whisper, "You're welcome."

I scoot past her and make for my car.

My shaky hand makes it impossible to get my keys into the ignition.

I roll the pill in my other hand faster.

Take it, Nick. Make this go away. Please.

My fingers squeeze together and the pill crushes to powder, floating to the floor of the car like ash.

I cry and laugh all at once the entire way home.

Epilogue (One Year Later)

"I want you to say it," Lori looks at me and waits. "I'm a published author."

I kick my feet and wiggle where I stand. Lori has been my teacher for a little over a year now, helping me with my writing whenever she can. I have a full manuscript under my belt now and another one waiting to be written. In addition, I have just received confirmation that I've gotten a few writing submissions into the yearly college art magazine. It isn't much, but Lori thinks differently.

Her green eyes look gentle, but I can tell they aren't going to move.

"I'm a published writer," I say like a mouse. Though most of her students have already left to go home, a few are still packing and watch me from their seats. I scan the classroom, embarrassed, and meet her eyes again.

She nods her head.

"Okay, good. But I want you to say it again. Louder, so I can feel it."

I groan.

Since that initial meeting with her in her office, I had gone home every day and written like a possessed journalist. Every week I brought in chapters, had Lori read them, and went home to keep writing. Simply put, she made me find the part of me that still wanted to be a writer, even after I had thought I buried it away.

My eyes dance about the room. My laugh sounds nervous. There is no way out of this.

"I'm a published author," I say louder.

She grins.

"There you go. I'm proud of you, Nick."

I scratch my head. "An author in a college-run arts magazine with a couple of poems—" I say rolling my eyes.

"It's a start," she says as she begins packing her things into her bag. "It's so amazing how far you've come in just this last year, you know that?"

I nod my head, but can't keep eye contact.

I'm not good with compliments.

Her voice pauses until I look up.

"You got a cute baby sister. You quit that horrible job at Pepsi and got a job you love. And," she says as her eyebrows arch and her eyes grow large, "you wrote an entire book! All in a year! There are kids I've taught in master courses in universities that don't do that much!" Her face is lit up like a Christmas tree. She *really* is proud of me.

I'm blushing.

The book she was referring to was the one I had her help me on last summer. The one I had pitched to Travis so long ago. Each week she met with me and we'd go over our writings. I read her manuscript for a book she wanted to publish, and she would go over mine. She would go through and point out everything I did right, and everything I did wrong. She was honest, and in that honesty she gave me something I knew I had all along—what my friends and family knew to be true. She believed in me, and for once, I listened. She was the cheerleader in my brain.

Unfortunately, after I completed the novel, I got back into my old groove. She never found out that I hadn't tried to submit it to any agent or editor, and I was too embarrassed to tell her.

I was scared of failure.

Last year, when the woman had hugged me at Borders, praising me for how I had changed her life, I began forming the fleeting idea to write a young-adult memoir of my life. It seemed like such a dumb idea, but I brought it up to Lori anyway.

She loved it, but I was reserved. Everyone wrote a sappy autobiography nowadays, so what was so special about my own?

On the bright side, she gave me the encouragement I needed so desperately.

"Thanks, Lori."

"You're done with the draft of the autobiography you're writing? You've put so much effort into thinking out the outline. I'm telling you, you're a shoo-in with that thing."

"Almost," I half lie. As dumb as I think the idea is, I am still attempting to write it. I truly do want to write about how I beat the odds. Encourage others to do the same. But now, halfway through writing it, I realize that I have not become the writer I always dreamed of. There is no point to the story if, in the end, nothing has changed. I still hate everything I write. There is nothing extraordinary about my life.

"I'm so very proud of you," she repeats to herself as she finishes her packing, just loud enough so I can hear it. "Goodnight, Nick. Keep writing. Don't give up."

"Goodnight." I smile and walk away.

She is more than my teacher, she is my mentor and my friend.

She makes me take compliments even if I don't want to.

I should have hugged her for that.

⤳

The Word document on my screen is completely blank. My fingers hover over the keys. The desk next to me is one large pile of scattered papers. Stacked on the very top of all the sloppy mounds, I have all the chapters I have written so far for my autobiography.

On the way home from Lori's class, I had the sudden burst of inspiration to finish it. Her words put me into a high and the entire drive home, my brain had flooded with ideas and plots and twists. I believed in myself.

But as I soon as I sat down and booted my laptop, the blank screen welcomed the same emotions that had forced me to give up so many times before.

I have no idea what to write. Where to start and what to say.

I pound my fist on the desk.

I can do this!

Lori believes in me. My family and friends believe in me. I can do this, dammit! My head falls to the keyboard. So much for positive affirmations.

"Maybe everyone's wrong," I say aloud. "Maybe I'm not a good writer. I mean, what's so special about my story?" I throw my hands up. "Everyone has a bad childhood story to tell. And everyone writes a book about it! What makes my story so unique?"

I know the answer. It isn't unique. It isn't special. There are hundreds of stories better than mine.

My story isn't worth telling because who in their right mind will care? Some kid loses his dream, loses himself in drugs, and digs himself out. Can you say cliché? Can you say tired storyline?

I hear a thud on my door and I raise my head. I watch as the knob jiggles up and down. From behind the closed door I hear soft grunting sounds.

It pops open and Noel tumbles in.

She looks up to me and grins. She's such a happy child. Always smiling, and it is a gorgeous smile. All her teeth are grown in now and when she smiles, she keeps her jaw perfectly aligned and her teeth clamp together as though they are glued. As she bounces toward me, her hair wobbles back and forth. Mom has separated her black hair into two offshoots that make her look like a Chinese version of Pippi Longstocking.

She stops in front of me in her tiny pajamas, holding the pink blanket she carries everywhere with an iron grip.

"Hey there, Noel." I try not to sound defeated.

"Hi, Nick!" Her words are so clear now that every time I hear them I am taken back. She has really grown up this last year.

"I sleep." She points out toward the hall. "My room."

I laugh.

"Night, night Nick!" She crooks her tiny head and drops her blanket. "Hug?"

I bend from my chair and hold out my arms. She giggles and waddles into them. I squeeze and shake her until she lets out an infectious string of laughter.

"Goodnight," I whisper.

She wiggles out of my grasp and grabs her blanket. She races out of the room.

Funny how it works out.

We save her.

And she saves me in return.

I sit back down at my computer and don't even have a chance to glance at it before Noel comes dashing back in.

"Kiss! Kiss!" she yells, her eyes as large as quarters.

I bend down and give her a kiss. She quickly turns her head and sneaks another kiss onto my cheek.

She giggles and turns to leave.

I let out a large sigh and begin typing.

Maybe it is a story worth telling after all.

LaVergne, TN USA
20 January 2010
170657LV00007B/5/P